Rec'd '/80

International
Trade

© 1980

PERSPECTIVES ON ECONOMICS SERIES

Michael L. Wachter & Susan M. Wachter, Editors

PUBLISHED

FORTHCOMING

International Trade

Stephen P. Magee
University of Texas at Austin

ADDISON-WESLEY PUBLISHING COMPANY
Reading, Massachusetts • Menlo Park, California
London • Amsterdam • Don Mills, Ontario • Sydney

To my grandfather

Library of Congress Cataloging in Publication Data

Magee, Stephen P
    International trade.

    (Perspectives on economics)
    Includes index.
    1. Commerce. 2. International economic relations.
I. Title. II. Series.
HF1007.M29   382   78-74686
ISBN 0-201-08365-5

ISBN 0-201-08365-5
ABCDEFGHIJK-AL-89876543210

Foreword

The PERSPECTIVES ON ECONOMICS series has been developed to present economics students with up-to-date policy-oriented books written by leading scholars in this field. Many professors and students have stressed the need for flexible, contemporary materials that provide an understanding of current policy issues.

In general, beginning students in economics are not exposed to the controversial material and development of current issues that are the basis of research in economics. Because of their length and breadth of coverage, textbooks tend to lack current economic thinking on policy questions; in attempting to provide a balanced viewpoint, they often do not give the reader a feel for the lively controversy in each field. With this series, we have attempted to fill this void.

The books in this series are designed to complement standard text-books. Each volume reflects the research interests and views of the authors. Thus these books can also serve as basic reading material in the specific topic courses covered by each. The stress throughout is on the careful development of institutional factors and policy in the context of economic theory. Yet the exposition is designed to be accessible to undergraduate students and interested laypersons with an elementary background in economics.

Michael L. Wachter
Susan M. Wachter

Preface

I am grateful to a number of individuals for assistance in the preparation of this book: Gunter Richter prepared the sections on economic imperialism and the political theory of economic integration; Ross van Wassenhove provided research assistance on many topics, especially transportation, and helped prepare the bibliographies; and Jayne McCullough typed the manuscript at least twice.

My interest in international trade was first inspired by Charles P. Kindleberger. The interested reader should see his many works, especially *Foreign Trade and the National Economy*. I am also indebted to Jagdish Bhagwati for his work on the theory of distortions and to the late Harry G. Johnson for his work on distortions and international commercial policy.

This book was also influenced by my grandfather, Lester L. Brock, 1891–1978. He was a crusty old Texas rancher who gave me some good advice: "Study hard so you can get a good desk job when you grow up." This book is affectionately dedicated to him.

University of Texas at Austin
September 1979   S.M.

Contents

x   Contents

LIST OF TABLES

LIST OF FIGURES

Introduction

In 1295 Marco Polo returned to Venice after twenty-four years in Asia. His tales of asbestos, silk, cotton, sandalwoods, taffetas, pearls, and stones that burned (coal) expanded Europe's vision of the gains from international trade. Subsequent trade in these goods between Europe and the Far East illustrate five important motivations for international trade: new markets, new ideas, cheap labor, natural resources, and exotic products. Six hundred years later, these motivations are still powerful determinants of international trade. This book explores various economic theories and empirical evidence of international trading patterns.

Chapter 1 develops several background issues. These include the law of one price, the importance of transportation costs, the law of the declining share of foreign trade, the laws of concentration, and a short discussion of the gains from international trade. Because of decreases in transportation costs and reductions in tariffs, international trade has expanded more rapidly than world production as a whole since World War II. For the past twenty-five years, international trade has grown nearly twice as fast as gross national product in the free world. Of course international trade is not the only means by which differences in supply and demand can be alleviated. If the basic factors of production (capital, labor, etc.) are free to move, then movement of production to the market provides an alternative to international product trade. Location theory provides an explanation of when it is most efficient to move the factors of production and when it is most efficient to move the final product.

Chapter 2 examines international trade in standardized products. Several theories of comparative advantage attempt to explain *why* certain countries will export certain products and import others. The traditional Ricardo model is discussed along with the more recent Heckscher-Ohlin model. These theories of comparative advantage occupy the centerpiece of most books on international trade, but my own opinion is that they are overrated. The history of postwar international trade theory has been one of attempting to patch up either the Ricardo or the Heckscher-Ohlin model in order to fit the facts as we know them. While we have gained considerable understanding in this undertaking, the experience has been an arduous one. The traditional theories of international advantage are strongest in explaining trade in products for which production technology is fairly well defined and unchanging. The Ricardo model has had some success empirically but it is extremely limited in asserting that goods are produced with only one factor of production, labor. High output-labor ratios are correlated with export success across industries, but this is quite possibly due to unmeasured inputs or other determinants of export success (see Bhagwati, 1964). The Heckscher-Ohlin model is more realistic in assuming the presence of both capital and labor as inputs into the product production process, but about half of the empirical tests reject its ability to correctly predict trade patterns. Furthermore, both the Ricardo and the Heckscher-Ohlin models adopt the very restrictive assumption that the production technology for a product does not change over the relevant time horizon. This has led Hufbauer (1966) and others to conclude that these theories of comparative advantage are most appropriate for "low-wage trade," meaning that the theories work only for those products with highly standardized production technology (so that unskilled laborers are important in production).

Successful empirical explanations of international trade in new products are provided by the alternative theories discussed in Chapter 3. Theories explaining international trade in raw materials are discussed in Chapter 4. For these two important types of international trade—high technology and raw materials—the traditional theory of comparative advantage is dominated by more current ones.

International trade in new products can be explained by a variety of theories: In addition to comparative advantage, these include imperfect competition, appropriability, the capital market approach, and the Vernon product cycle. The latter has generated considerable discussion since its publication in the mid-1960s. It is a rich and provocative hypothesis built squarely upon the stylized facts.

Chapter 4 on raw materials discusses international commodity agreements, "shortages" in "exhaustible" resources, research and development as a substitute for international trade, and a raw materials product cycle. This product cycle parallels the Vernon product cycle for manufactured goods. However, the raw materials cycle is the reverse of the Vernon product cycle in that production moves from developing countries early in the "life" of a primary product and eventually is replaced by the production of synthetics or high technology alternatives in developed countries later.

Is there a theory of comparative advantage that applies to both low- and high-technology manufactured products as well as to raw materials? I would like to suggest a "product age theory of comparative advantage": *Young manufactured products are produced in developed countries, while old manufactured products are produced in developing countries; young raw materials are produced in developing countries, while older raw materials are produced in developed countries.* The manufactured product generalization comes from Vernon (1966), while the raw materials part of the theory has been developed by Magee and Robins (1978). The empirical implications of this theory are that knowledge of production location requires only knowledge of product age, whether it is a manufactured good or a raw material. Notice that the traditional theory of comparative advantage covers a narrow range of trade and applies primarily only to the last stage in the Vernon product cycle (old manufactured products). The product age theory is not discussed in the text; I mention it here to provide an integrative force and perspective for the reading of Chapters 2, 3, and 4.

Chapter 5 investigates the impact of international trade on the primary factors of production, capital and labor. The factor price equalization theorem, the Stolper-Samuelson theorem, the Cairnes model, and the Rybczynski theorem are all investigated. The effects of labor unions and other distortions in factor markets on patterns of international trade are also considered. The chapter concludes with a discussion of migration theory, a case in which the factor moves to the market.

Chapter 6, the concluding chapter, discusses five issues relating politics and international trade. The first concerns the theory of tariffs and their costs and benefits. The second relates economic and political considerations to economic integration: When do countries coalesce into larger political and economic units such as the European Common Market? The third issue is a country's balance of trade: What are the reasons for imbalances and what are the political and economic effects of them? For example, the Chinese-British Opium Wars in the 1840s are closely related to trade imbalances which developed over several centuries between Britain, India, and the Far East. A fourth issue is economic imperialism: Why and how do advanced countries attempt to exploit raw materials suppliers? The final issue is international trade and economic development: Subsidiary issues include the relationship between manufactured exports and development, the tendency for export earnings by developing countries to fluctuate more than those in developed countries, and downward ratchets in the terms of trade of developing countries.

REFERENCES

1. Bhagwati, Jagdish, "The Pure Theory of International Trade: A Survey," *Economic Journal* **74** (March 1964): 1–84.

2. Hufbauer, Gary C., *Synthetic Materials and the Pure Theory of International Trade*. Cambridge: Harvard University Press, 1966.

3. Magee, Stephen P. and Robins, Norman I., "The Raw Material Product Cycle," in Krause, Lawrence B. and Patrick, Hugh, eds., *Mineral Resources in the Pacific Area*. San Francisco: Federal Reserve Bank of San Francisco, 1978: 30–55.

4. Vernon, Raymond, "International Investment and International Trade in the Product Cycle," *Quarterly Journal of Economics* **80** (May 1966): 190–207.

International 1
Trade,
Transportation
Costs, and
the Law of
One Price

This chapter examines five preliminary matters that are necessary to an understanding of international trade. Section 1.1 examines the single most important principle underlying international trade theory—the law of one price. The pressure for goods, factors, and services to flow from low-price regions to high-price regions is inexorable. Section 1.2 considers the cost of international transportation. Whether goods move or factors move depends on the relative cost of moving each. Section 1.3 discusses the law of the declining share of foreign trade with respect to the size of each country and economic activity. There are economic forces that reduce the importance of foreign trade for large economies; smaller economies are more dependent on the outside world for their economic livelihood. Section 1.4 discusses the law of concentration in trade: Countries export fewer products than they import. This tendency gets stronger the lower the per capita income of the country. Finally, Section 1.5 examines the gains from international trade. The benefit to a country from engaging in international trade derives both from the availability of new products on world markets at low prices and from producers spending more time specializing in what they do well.

1.1 THE LAW OF ONE PRICE

The law of one price is a restatement of the principle that one should buy cheap and sell dear. This process will continue until prices, adjusted transportation costs, tariffs, and other barriers, are equalized among economies. The law of one price certainly applies to commodities: They move from regions where they are abundant and cheap to regions where they are scarce and dear. It also applies to factors of production. For example, if there is a dramatic and unpredicted increase in pollution in an area, some labor will leave the area for more hospitable surroundings. This principle is so pervasive that almost every principle in international trade theory can be related to it.

International Trade in Laws and Taxes

Market forces cause the economic base of high-tax countries to gravitate toward low-tax countries. Multinational corporations, when possible, locate offices and production facilities in tax-haven countries such as the Bahamas, Liechtenstein, and certain cantons of Switzerland, to minimize their annual tax payments. This hurts high-tax countries and helps low-tax countries. If the factors of production (capital and labor) are sufficiently mobile, high-tax countries face erosion of their tax base, which places downward pressure on their taxes; low-tax countries can raise their taxes without much loss of the base. International tax rates are thereby moved together.

The law of one price also applies to laws and other societal con-straints. For example, illegal activities are moved from areas in which they are heavily penalized to areas where the law is more lenient. In the 1920s, Al Capone moved from Chicago, where his activities had come under close scrutiny, to Cicero, Illinois, where a more favorable climate existed. Similarly, consumers of illegal drugs move from areas of tight prosecution to areas in which sanctions are less stringent. One wag observed that since the Soviet Union appears to have a comparative advantage in cruel and unusual punishment, the United States should export its hardened criminals there. Explanation of this empirical depar-ture from the law of one price for international trade in retribution is left as an exercise for the reader.

International Trade in Warehouses?

The law of one price applies even to international trade in such immobile items as warehouses. For example, it is not uncommon for the "date of order" on U.S. customs documents to be later than the "date of shipment" from Japan. The high cost of warehousing in Japan induces producers to load excess inventories and goods with recurring orders on freighters coming to the United States. When orders are received for the goods, the order is relayed to the ship by radio and the items can be unloaded at the nearest U.S. port. Even if an order is not received by the time a boat reaches its last port of disembarcation, the goods can usually be stored in American warehouses more cheaply than in Japanese warehouses. Thus the Japanese have engaged in arbitrage of international warehousing services. This practice has several indirect costs, including economic sanctions levied by the United States against "dumping"; that is, selling goods in the United States below Japanese prices.

Evidence on the Law of One Price

It is obvious that people will buy where items are cheap and sell where they are dear. It is also obvious that items will be cheap where they are abundant and more expensive where they are rare. Somewhat less obvious is the fact that the prices of homogeneous commodities, after all taxes have been subtracted, will be equalized internationally up to the costs of transportation. Even this statement must be modified when anti-competitive elements are present, since a monopolist will charge higher prices in markets that view the good as "a necessity" (i.e., the quantity purchased is less responsive to price) than in markets that do not.

The data in Table 1.1 show that the price of regular gasoline, after import taxes (duties) and domestic taxes are subtracted, ranges from an average of less than 20 cents a gallon in oil-producing countries to about 65 cents a gallon in Europe. There is mild evidence that the net prices of gasoline are related to the distance of a country from an oil producer. For example, Tunisia buys oil from its neighbor Libya.

At the same time, wine is similar to gasoline in that it is cheapest in areas of largest production. Paris, Milan, Lisbon, and Madrid are the low-price places in the world to consume wine. In 1977, a medium quality table wine could be purchased in these cities for 52¢ to 65¢ a bottle. There are many examples where market arbitrage is unrelated to distance. For example, men's clothing is a bargain in London and Milan, where it is approximately one-half of the U.S. price, but in Paris, it usually costs more than in the United States. There is less arbitrage internationally in taxi rides. A three-mile taxi ride in San Francisco in 1977 cost $4.20 plus tip, making it the highest in the world; the same ride in either Athens or Madrid was less than $1.10.

When all items, including both international tradables and non-tradables are included, there are substantial differences in prices. In 1977, a representative market basket of food, clothing, transportation, services, and appliances ranged from $820 in Tokyo (the most expensive) to $620 in New York to $420 in London. Manama (the capital of Bahrain), Oslo, Stockholm, Zurich, Geneva, Copenhagen, and Tel Aviv were all more expensive than New York, while Madrid and Milan are less expensive than London. Thus, although there are market pressures toward price equalizations, differences can persist for long periods of time.

Table 1.1 Price per gallon of regular gasoline, 1976

Location	U.S. cents per U.S. gallon			
	Retail price	Duty	Tax	Price net of duty and taxes
Europe				
Belgium	143.0	74.0	8.0	61.0
Denmark	140.0	53.0	18.0	69.0
France	140.0	-	75.6	64.4
Germany	138.6	4.3	65.6	68.7
Greece	159.1	3.6	91.2	64.3
Italy	169.8	4.1	110.2	55.5
Luxembourg	117.5	51.4	5.6	60.5
Norway	151.2	-	98.2	53.0
Portugal	180.7	40.6	88.4	51.7
Spain	121.0	-	33.0	88.0
Switzerland	.150.0	81.0	5.0	64.0
United Kingdom	125.1	53.4	15.0	56.6
Oil-producing countries				
Iran	32.2	-	-	32.2
Saudi Arabia	11.8	-	-	11.8
Venezuela	13.8	-	1.8	12.0
Near and Far East				
India	142.4	90.1	9.9	42.4
Israel	164.0	50.0	60.0	54.0
Pakistan	100.8	33.3	53.3	14.2
Philippines	71.0	1.5	16.8	52.7
Thailand	76.8	20.8	3.2	52.8
Latin America				
Argentina	96.6	43.0	40.3	13.3
Mexico	65.0	-	22.0	43.0
Peru	77.0	-	37.0	40.0
Uruguay	140.0	-	61.0	79.0
Africa				
Kenya	109.0	27.0	18.0	64.0
Morocco	146.0	6.6	90.5	48.9
South Africa	98.3	34.0	-	64.3
Tunisia	147.4	-	117.2	30.2
Other developed countries				
Japan	136.1	2.7	56.7	76.7
United States	59.9	1.3	12.0	46.6

Source: Calculated from the *International Petroleum Annual*, March, 1977, Table 10, 30- 36.

1.2 TRANSPORTATION COSTS

Barriers between country markets weaken the law of one price. If it costs 30 percent of the British value of a good to transport it to the United States, then U.S. prices can be up to 30 percent higher than U.K. prices, and still it will not be profitable to ship the goods to the United States. The *economic distance* between two points in the world is related to transportation costs per ton mile as well as distance. For international trade as a whole, total transportation costs average from 10 to 15 percent of the value of the product. There is obviously considerable variation around this average; precious jewels have a low ratio of transportation cost to value, while real estate has nearly an infinite ratio.

Modes of transportation also vary between intracountry trade and international trade. Table 1.2 shows that truck and rail account for 63 percent of U.S. domestic ton miles, whereas only 27 percent of the value of U.S. exports are transported by these modes. Vessels account for only 16 percent of U.S. domestic transportation, while 56 percent of U.S. exports go by vessel. Furthermore, the use of domestic vessel shipments is highly concentrated in certain areas: Forty-one percent of water traffic consists of petroleum; 17 percent is coal and coke; 13 percent is sand, gravel, and stone; and 10 percent is iron ore, iron, and steel (Locklin, 1972, p. 722). Air freight is also much more important for U.S. exports (17 percent) than for domestic transportation (1 percent).

If you shipped 100,000 pounds of books from New York to Houston in 1978, it would have cost you $5700 by truck, $6800 by rail and $62,000 by air freight. Air freight is fast but it is 10 times more expensive than either truck or rail. Truck dominates rail transportation both because of price and convenience; for this size shipment, trucking usually provides door-to-door service at both the origin and the destination. Rail transport is probably more efficient only for much larger shipments.

What have been the most important breakthroughs in international shipping in the last century? Innovations in international transport have included the opening of the Suez Canal in 1869, adaptation of steam engines and screw propellers to ironclad vessels in the 1870s, refrigeration of ships in the 1880s, tanker ships, completion of the Panama Canal in 1914; and more recently, containerized ships and international pipelines.

There is another aspect of transportation that is important. If all commodities could be efficiently produced within 10 miles of each consumer, then international trade would be unimportant. However, many raw materials are concentrated geographically: Malaysia has 37 percent of the world's tin; the United States has 47 percent of the world's magnesium; and Zaïre has 57 percent of the world's cobalt. Thus *it is the geographical*

Table 1.2 Modes of transportation for U.S. domestic and foreign trade

| Mode of transportation | Dollars per ton | Gross revenues and miles hauled for freight in the United States, 1975* | | Value of U.S. exports by method of transport, 1977 |
		Billions of dollars of revenue	Billions of ton miles	Billions of dollars
Rail	.020	16.5 (12%)	796 (37%)	32 (27%)
Truck	.223	109.7 (71%)	490 (26%)	67 (56%)
Vessel	.022	8.0 (6%)	352 (16%)	20 (17%)
Air	.450	1.8 (1%)	4 (1%)	
Total of Above		136.0 (100%)	1642 (100%)	119 (100%)

Source: Transportation Association of America, "Transportation Facts & Trends," 13th ed., 1974.

mismatching of resources and the factors of production with markets that generates the need for international trade. But international trade in commodities is only one solution: The mismatching problem could also be remedied by movement of resources and factors to the market. Whether trade in final goods or trade in factors satisfies the market is affected by the economic costs of moving each. A schematic chart of these possibilities and the conceptual approaches to each is shown in Fig. 1.1. In case 1, the high cost of moving factors and low cost of moving commodities generate international trade in commodities, a phenomenon that is explained by *international trade theory.* In case 2, the high cost of moving commodities and low cost of moving factors of production make it most economical for production to be located at the market. *Migration theory* is used to describe international movements of labor, while the *theory of foreign direct investment* describes movement of physical capital in the world. The theory of foreign direct investment will be examined in Chapter 3 and migration theory will be examined in Chapter 5. Cases 3, 4, and 5 are best described by the *location theory.* In case 3, low-cost transportation makes the decision of where to locate dependent upon other considerations; this situation is called *footloose production* since it can occur anywhere. In case 5, no international trade occurs in either commodities or factors because of high transportation costs. Two economies that do not engage in international transactions with each other, because of transportation costs or for any other reason, are said to be in a state of *autarky.*

We know which form of analysis to apply to international economic transactions based on transportation costs. However, these transactions must occur between geographically separate economic regions. But what is an "economic region"? In 1923, Bertil Ohlin defined an economic region as areas "within which the factors of production move freely but between which they are completely immobile." The European Economic Community is an example of an economic region since the European countries are eliminating politically imposed barriers to the movement of factors. The United States would have somewhat more difficulty in qualifying as an economic region since there are no significant politically imposed barriers to movements of capital and labor within the United States. Nevertheless, the long distances involved impose economic barriers that may make New York City closer to Nova Scotia than to Los Angeles for many transactions. It should be clear that the definition of an economic region is not an absolute.

Location Theory

The question addressed by location theory is where to locate production for goods that use raw material inputs. Should production be located at the site of the raw material (e.g., at the ore source for steel production) or

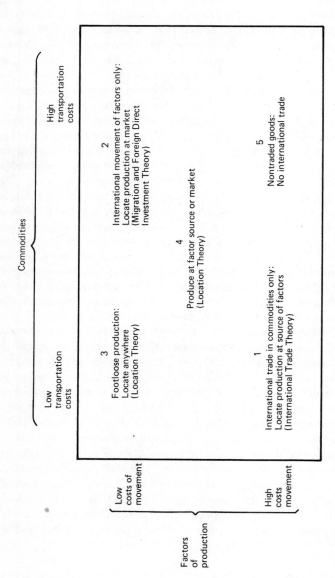

Fig. 1.1 Theories explaining movements of factors and commodities

should it be located at the market (e.g., near automobile plants and other consumers of steel)? The implications for international trade are that we will observe more international trade in the final products (steel) if production is located at the raw material source, while we will observe international trade in the raw material (iron ore) if production is located at the market.

The goal of location theory is to choose production location so as to minimize total transportation costs; it largely ignores other consider- ations, such as costs of capital, labor, and other nonmaterial inputs. There are three important considerations in determining which production location will minimize transportation costs: the spatial distribution of raw materials, the extent to which the production process is weight-losing or weight-gaining, and the extent to which transportation costs per ton mile differ between raw material inputs and the final product.

Consider first the spatial distribution of raw materials. Raw materials are *localized* if they exist at only a few scattered locations. Deposits of coal minerals and petroleum are usually localized. A raw material is *ubiquitous* if it is widely distributed and available at most potential production locations. Air is ubiquitous. Land and water are usually ubiquitous although they vary considerably in quality and quantity. Of course neither of these can be uniquely classified since any given resource varies from region to region. For example, water is ubiquitous in many countries but it is highly localized in desert regions. Rainfall occurs everywhere but is localized with respect to quantity: The island of Maui in the Hawaiian Islands has recorded an annual rainfall of 562 inches, but the Sahara Desert can go for long periods with no rainfall at all. Other things being equal, producers are under fewer constraints in their location decision for products using ubiquitous raw materials than for products using localized raw materials.

A second important consideration is whether the production process involves weight loss or weight gain. For example, when iron ore is converted into pig iron, there is a weight loss: It requires two tons of iron ore to obtain a ton of pig iron (Smith, 1971, p. 356). In contrast, the production of soft drinks is a weight-gaining process since water is added to the basic flavorings and syrup at the time soft drinks are bottled. If transportation costs per ton mile are identical for the raw material input and the final product, then production tends to be located at the source of the raw material for weight-losing processes and at the product market for weight-gaining processes.

The third consideration is whether transportation costs differ be- tween raw materials and the final product. For example, it is probably cheaper to haul a ton of iron ore than an assembled automobile weighing one ton due to higher density of the ore and less care required in handling. One study showed that transportation costs per ton mile for finished steel were three times higher than for coal and four times higher than for iron ore (Smith, 1971, p. 348). If transportation costs per ton mile of the raw material are sufficiently lower than those of the final product, they will offset the heavier weight of the raw material and dictate that production be located at the final product market.

1.3   THE LAW OF THE DECLINING SHARE OF FOREIGN TRADE OF FOREIGN TRADE

The Declining Share of Trade with Respect to Country Size

There are two laws of the declining share of foreign trade. The first law suggests that the larger the geographic size of a country, the smaller foreign trade will be as a proportion of gross national product. There are two reasons for this phenomenon. First, if a region is small enough, then nearly all of its trade will be with the outside. For example, if we define the world to be one country, there would clearly be no outside trade. The law of the declining share of trade with respect to country size is partly therefore a mathematical inevitability.

But there is another reason—transportation and distribution costs. For example, if the maximum radius for bread distribution is 100 miles, then a larger proportion of bread will be supplied by local than by international trade for the United States compared to Monaco. The more important transportation costs are, the more a large country must depend upon local supply.

The empirical evidence for this law is shown in Fig. 1.2. Note the steady decline in the average size of the countries as the share of foreign trade in national income increases. The United States, Brazil, and India all have shares of foreign trade in national income which are less than 10 percent. Small countries, such as the Netherlands, Ireland, and Iceland, have international trade in excess of 40 percent of their national income.

The Declining Share of Trade with Respect to Economic Activity

The second law of the declining share of foreign trade suggests that as income per capita in a country of a particular geographical size grows, foreign trade as a proportion of national income will decline. The evidence to support this theory is weak and has been established only for developed countries. Still, there are several arguments for the theory. First, the income elasticity of demand for food falls above certain income levels. Countries that are import dependent on food will have a decline in the relative importance of such imports as they grow. Second, early in the

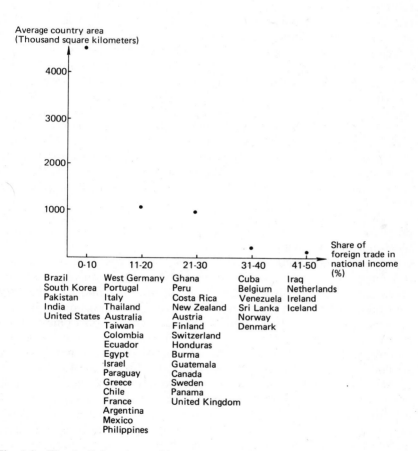

Fig. 1.2 The declining share of international commodity trade with respect to country size

development stage, countries expend large amounts on social overhead capital (roads, parks, schools, etc.). Construction is important in building this type of capital, and foreign trade is unimportant in most construction activities. Third, the service sector becomes increasingly important as an economy develops: Legal, medical, government, and transportation services all increase as a proportion of national income. With the exception of international travel, these activities use relatively small inputs of internationally traded goods. Since consumption of goods of all types decreases with respect to the income because of this phenomenon, the relative importance of foreign trade can also be expected to decrease. Fourth, the development of sophisticated and skilled-labor forces permits local economies to provide a wider variety of goods than were formerly available. If the capability and desire of local labor to provide wider variety grows faster than local demand for a wider variety of goods, then dependence on foreign trade decreases. Fifth, the increasing importance of research and development in developed countries permits them to economize on imports of scarce raw materials and to replace them with synthetics (see Chapter 4).

The preceding theory has detectable, though weak, empirical support. The most important theoretical qualification to the theory is provided by Johnson's distinction between the behavior of production versus consumption as income grows. Imports of any goods equal domestic consumption less domestic production. If consumption of beef grows much more rapidly than income and if beef is imported, then the consumption effect can be expected to stimulate increasing imports of beef. However, whether actual imports increase depends on domestic production. In the postwar period, domestic production of beef has grown more rapidly than domestic consumption so that beef imports have actually declined in absolute terms. Thus any discussion of the share of trade in a national economy must be made with simultaneous investigation of consumption and production. An argument similar to the one above but with the arguments reversed applies to exports since they equal domestic production less domestic consumption. Whenever production rises more rapidly than consumption, exports are stimulated and foreign trade in the national economy will increase for this particular product.

1.4   THE LAW OF CONCENTRATION

Individuals usually consume a much wider variety of goods and services than they produce. The same is true of countries: We observe that they have a much more diversified structure of imports than of exports. There appear to be two systematic laws of concentration.

The first law of concentration states that *exports are more concentrated for developing countries than for developed countries.* Developing economies have a narrower range of skills than do highly developed industrial economies. For this reason, they have a larger proportion of their total exports in a single commodity. Table 1.3 shows the share of the major export in total 1974 exports. Notice that the average share of the principal commodity in exports is 54 percent for the developing countries but only 17 percent for the developed countries. This is one frequently cited reason why developing countries experience wider fluctuations in their export earnings than do industrial economies. Any country that specializes in a single product tends to tie its export earnings directly to the fortunes of the world market in that product. If world demand falls for this commodity, then the export earnings of that economy fall as well. More highly developed economies are less subject to this problem since products that have short falls in some product areas can always be offset by gains in other products. This product diversification is less possible for the developing economies, which specialize in fewer products.

The second law of concentration is the following: *Half of the developing countries earn half or more of their export revenues from a single commodity.* This is simply an empirical rule of thumb derived from Table 1.3. Notice that about half of the developing countries have more than 50 percent of their exports in a single two-digit commodity, while the other half have less than 50 percent. We will consider the implications of commodity specialization for international commodity agreements and for economic development in Chapters 4 and 6.

1.5   THE GAINS FROM TRADE

Any country that engages in international trade derives two advantages: economic welfare increases because of consumption as well as production gains. Consider first the consumption gain. Consumers in the United States are better off being able to purchase on world markets products that are less expensive than those at home. For example, if it costs $12.07 to produce and market a pair of shoes made in New England, but the same shoe can be imported from Italy at $4.18, American consumers benefit by being allowed to purchase on world markets. Italian consumers also benefit by being allowed to purchase on world markets (e.g., Italian consumers can obtain sophisticated capital equipment from the United States at a lower price than they can produce it in their country). Since there is always a set of goods that will cost more abroad and a set of goods that cost less, consumers in any market benefit by free international trade.

Table 1.3   Share of principal commodity in 1974 exports[1]

Country	SITC code	Commodity	Principal commodity as % of total exports
Developing countries			
Libya	33	petroleum and products	99
Netherlands Antilles	33	petroleum and products	96
Nigeria	33	petroleum and products	93
Trinidad and Tobago	33	petroleum and products	90
Reunion	06	sugar and prep'ns, honey	81
Uganda	07	coffee, tea, cocoa, spices	78
Jamaica	28	metalliferous ores, scrap	74
Ghana	07	coffee, tea, cocoa, spices	73
Chile	68	nonferrous metals	73
Indonesia	33	petroleum and products	70
Liberia	28	metalliferous ores, scrap	66
Sierra Leone	66	nonmetal mineral mfg., misc.	63
Iceland	03	fish and prep'ns	61
Morocco	27	crude fertilizers, minerals, misc.	55
Dominican Republic	06	sugar and prep'ns, honey	55
Martinique	05	fruits and vegetables	52
Niger	28	metalliferous ores, scrap	50
Guadeloupe	05	fruits and vegetables	48
Ivory Coast	07	coffee, tea, cocoa, spices	48
Egypt	26	textile fibers	48
Cyprus	05	fruits and vegetables	48
Colombia	07	coffee, tea, cocoa, spices	44
Madagascar	07	coffee, tea, cocoa, spices	44
Malawi	12	tobacco and mfgs.	44
Burma	04	cereals and prep'ns	42
Sudan	26	textile fibers	38
Israel	66	nonmetal mineral mfg., misc.	36
Kenya	07	coffee, tea, cocoa, spices	36
Pakistan	65	textile yarn, fabric, etc.	34
Thailand	04	cereal and prep'ns	33
Finland	64	paper, paperboard, and mfg.	31
Philippines	06	sugar and prep'ns, honey	28
Malasia	231	crude rubber	28
Ethiopia	07	coffee, tea, cocoa, spices	28
Turkey	05	fruits and vegetables	22
Brazil	06	sugar and prep'ns, honey	17
Average			54

		Developed countries	
Japan	73	transport equipment	24
Switzerland	71	machinery, nonelectric	23
Germany	71	machinery, nonelectric	21
Norway	73	transport equipment	20
United Kingdom	71	machinery, nonelectric	19
Belgium-Luxembourg	67	iron and steel	18
United States	71	machinery, nonelectric	17
Sweden	71	machinery, nonelectric	16
Australia	04	cereals and prep'ns	16
Italy	71	machinery, nonelectric	16
Denmark	71	machinery, nonelectric	15
Austria	71	machinery, nonelectric	13
Netherlands	33	petroleum and products	13
France	73	transport equipment	12
Canada	33	petroleum and products	12
		Average	17

[1]Defined as the percentage share of the largest two-digit standard International Trade Classification commodity in the country's total exports in 1974.

Consider next the production gains from trade. Since some goods will always be higher on world markets than at home (even taking transportation costs into account), producers in each country benefit by being able to produce those goods in which they have some advantage over foreign producers. In general, an economy will cease to produce those goods that can be produced more cheaply abroad and increase their production of goods that are produced more expensively abroad. (See the discussion of the theory of comparative advantage in Chapter 2). The production gains from trade result from an economy switching its type of production toward goods in which it has the greatest comparative advantage.

REFERENCES

1. Bressler, Raymond G. and King, Richard A., *Markets, Prices, and Interregional Trade.* New York: John Wiley & Sons, 1970, Ch. 18.
2. Fryxell, David A., "International Economy: We're No. 1," *Ambassador* **10** (September 1977): 50.
3. Johnson, Harry G., *Money, Trade and Economic Growth.* Cambridge, Mass.: Harvard University Press, 1967, Ch. 4.
4. Kindleberger, Charles P., *Foreign Trade in the National Economy.* New Haven: Yale University Press, 1962, Chs. 2 and 11.

5. Magee, Stephen P., "U.S. Import Prices in the Currency-Contract Period," *Brookings Papers on Economic Activity* (No. 1, 1974): 129, footnote 8.

6. Michaely, Michael, *Concentration in International Trade*. Amsterdam: North-Holland, 1967.

7. Ohlin, Bertil, *Interregional and International Trade*. Cambridge, Mass.: Harvard University Press, 1933.

8. Smith, David M., *Industrial Location*. New York: John Wiley & Sons, 1971.

International 2
Trade in
Standardized
Products

After products become older and their production technology becomes known worldwide, costs of production become increasingly important in determining the best production location. As we shall see in the next chapter, it is important that production be located close to the market for new products for a while. With older, standardized products, this dependence of production location on market location weakens. Countries will produce and export products they can produce cheaply and import those they cannot produce cheaply. The various theories of comparative advantage attempt to explain *why* production costs are low in some countries and high in others. Frankly, these theories are not very good at explaining why specific products are produced in specific locations. A large number of international entrepreneurs have done quite well with little or no knowledge of the theory of comparative advantage.

The first theory to be considered is the Ricardo theory of comparative advantage, which assumes a single factor of production, labor, and is based on the labor theory of value developed in the 18th and 19th centuries. The second theory is the Heckscher-Ohlin model based on two factors of production, usually capital and labor.

2.1 THE RICARDO MODEL

The Labor Theory of Value

The labor theory of value states that the value of any product is equal to the value of the labor time required to produce it. For example, if an automobile requires two worker-years worth of labor to construct and a truck requires six worker-years, then the price of a truck will be three times as high as that of a car. We assume that the two worker-years required to produce a car include the amount of time taken to process the materials that go into the automobile.

The Ricardo Theory of Comparative Advantage

Ricardo used this labor theory of value to construct his theory of comparative advantage, which states that a country will produce and export products that use the lowest amount of labor time relative to foreign countries and import those products that have the highest amount of labor time in production relative to foreign countries. Furthermore, only *relative* amounts of labor time matter.

Table 2.1   Worker-years required for production (output per worker-year)

	United States	*Canada*
1 Car	2 (.5/year)	4 (.25/year)
1 Truck	6 (.17/year)	8 (.125/year)
Price of truck/Price of car	3/1	2/1

Consider the production time required to produce one car and one truck in the United States and in Canada (see Table 2.1). It requires two worker-years to produce a car and six worker-years to produce a truck in the United States. In Canada, it requires four worker-years to construct a car but eight worker-years to construct a truck. According to the labor theory of value, the price of trucks relative to cars will be three to one in the United States, but only two to one in Canada. According to Ricardo's theory, Canada will export trucks since they are relatively less expensive there, while the United States will export cars. Thus Canada produces only trucks for its own consumers and for customers in the United States, while the United States produces only cars, both for its local consumers and for Canadian consumers.

Before international trade was instituted between the United States and Canada, the price of trucks in the United States relative to cars was 3/1, whereas it was only 2/1 in Canada. After international trade opens up, we know that prices will be pushed together in the two markets (ignoring transportation costs). Americans will go to Canada and bid the relative price of trucks above 2/1 while Canadians will sell their trucks in the United States, reducing the U.S. price below 3/1. Eventually, an equilibrium will be reached with the world price of trucks somewhere between 2/1 and 3/1, say, 2.7/1. This result holds in any situation in which the trading partners are both sufficiently large to affect the price in the other market.

In the case of a very small country, such as Luxembourg, trading with a large country, such as the United States, the world price after international trade has opened up may be established at the price existing in the large country before trade started. For example, if we substitute Luxembourg for Canada in Table 2.1, it is possible that the world price after trade is opened up will still be 3/1. Even though Luxembourg will export trucks to the United States, it may hold such a small percentage of the U.S. market that the U.S. price will not fall noticeably. In this situation of a small country trading with a large one, all of the gains from international trade accrue to the small country. The United States gains little by having an economy only 1/1000th its size trading with it. However, it is a considerable advantage to Luxembourg since it is now able to import cars much more cheaply than it was able to produce them itself. This is a counterargument to the popular belief that large countries gain at the expense of small ones in international trade.

The Myth of Absolute Advantage

A cursory glance at Table 2.1 would lead one to believe that there would be no advantage for the United States to trade with Canada. The reason is that the United States can produce both cars and trucks using fewer worker-years than is possible in Canada. The United States can produce a car in half the time required in Canada and a truck in only 3/4 the time. However, one of Ricardo's important contributions was to debunk the myth of absolute advantage; that is, the notion that the United States should produce both products and not engage in international trade. This can be shown by examining whether workers in the United States who produce cars could gain by trading those cars for trucks in Canada. A U.S. worker can produce a car in two years. After working 12 years, that worker could take the resulting six cars and purchase two trucks in the U.S. Would there be any gain in taking these six cars to Canada and trading them there for trucks? Clearly there would be, since six cars in Canada can be exchanged for three trucks. Thus, even though U.S. workers are superior in both products, it pays them to specialize in the item in which they have the greatest relative advantage (cars) and trade them in Canada for trucks.

Empirical Evidence for the Ricardo Model

In parentheses in Table 2.1, we note the number of cars and trucks that can be produced per worker-year in each country. Notice that the ratio of labor productivity (output per worker) in the production of cars relative to trucks is 3/1 in the United States, while it is only 2/1 in Canada. This suggests a direct test of the theory. It should be true that countries will export products in which they have high relative labor productivity and import those products in which they have low relative labor productivity. The results of MacDougall's test of this theory (1951) are shown in Figure 2.1. The ratio of labor productivity in the United States to the labor productivity in the United Kingdom is shown on the vertical axis, and the ratio of U.S. exports to U.K. exports, both to third markets, is shown on the horizontal axis. Notice that for goods such as margarine, clothing, and rayon the ratio of U.S. output per worker relative to U.K. output per worker is small. For these items, the ratio of U.S. exports to U.K. exports is also small. However, for tin cans, pig iron, and automobiles, U.S. productivity is high relative to U.K. productivity and so are U.S. exports relative to U.K. exports. Thus it appears that this simple theory of relative advantage has impressive empirical support.

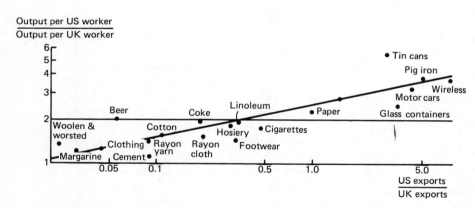

Fig. 2.1   Export performance related to labor productivity
Source: MacDougall (1951)

2.2   THE HECKSCHER-OHLIN MODEL

Despite the empirical success of the Ricardo model in explaining trade patterns, it is still unrealistic to believe that a model built on a single factor of production can explain international trade patterns. For this reason, a second model, which is based on two factors of production, has emerged. Each country is assumed to possess the two factors, capital and labor, and each product requires both of them in production. The Heckscher-Ohlin model suggests that countries will export products that use more of the country's abundant factor: Capital-abundant countries will export products that use a lot of capital in their production, that is, *capital-intensive* products, and labor-abundant countries will export *labor-intensive* products.

Assume that cars are more capital intensive in their production than trucks. This might be due to longer production runs on their assembly lines. Assume that it requires three units of capital per worker-year to assemble an automobile compared to only two units of capital per worker-year to assemble a truck. Assume also that the United States has more physical capital per worker than Canada. According to the Heckscher-Ohlin theorem, since the United States is relatively capital abundant, it will export its capital-intensive goods (cars). Canada will do the reverse; since it is relatively well endowed with labor, it will export the labor-intensive good (trucks). In contrast to the Ricardo model, in which each country produced only one good, both countries will produce both goods after free trade is opened. Thus, even though the United States is importing trucks, it will still satisfy some of the U.S. demand by producing trucks. The same is true for car production in Canada.

Before turning to empirical tests of the Heckscher-Ohlin theorem, some discussion of production in the United States and Canada is required. With free international trade, the prices of identical cars will be equated in the United States and Canada; the same will be true for trucks. By the factor of the price equalization theorem, the costs of capital and labor will also be equalized between the two countries because of free trade. When this is the case, within each industry the amounts of capital per worker used in production will be the same in Canada as in the United States. If we observe that 2.5 units of capital per worker are being used in car production in the United States, then 2.5 units of capital per worker will be used in car production in Canada. The same will be true for truck production; if 2.2 units of capital per worker are used in Canada, the same ratio will be used in the United States. If we are to test the Heckscher-Ohlin theorem, we must see if the relative capital intensity of exports matches the relative factor abundance of the economy. The first step is to establish whether the export good is more or less capital intensive in production than the import good. It is easy to measure capital intensity for U.S. exports: We simply calculate the dollar value of capital per worker in U.S. industries that produce goods for export. But do we measure capital intensity for U.S.

imports in the United States or in Canada? The point just made is that it does not matter whether we measure capital per worker in import-competing production of trucks in the United States or go to Canada and measure units of capital per worker in the production of trucks there.

Empirical Tests of the Heckscher-Ohlin Theorem Based on Capital and Labor

The United States. The most famous tests of the theorem were performed by Leontief in 1953 and 1956 on U.S. data. Because of the presumed physical abundance of capital relative to labor in the United States, the expectation was that the United States would export capital-intensive products and import labor-intensive products. Leontief's studies found that exactly the reverse was true. He found that in 1947, U.S. exports required $14,300 of capital per worker-year, while production that competed with U.S. imports required $18,200 worth of capital per worker-year. Input-output analysis was used to capture direct as well as indirect requirements of capital per worker in order to produce export and import-competing products. Given our preconception that the United States is capital abundant compared with the rest of the world, this test refutes the ability of the Heckscher-Ohlin model to predict the factor intensity of U.S. trade.

Japan. Given the abundance of labor in Japan relative to other factors, we would expect Japan to export labor-intensive products and import capital-intensive ones. A study by Tatemoto and Ichimura (1959) found the reverse: Japan exports capital-intensive goods but imports labor-intensive goods, contrary to the Heckscher-Ohlin predictions. On the other hand, whenever they broke Japanese trade into regions, they found that Japanese exports to the United States were labor-intensive relative to the imports from the United States. Vis-à-vis lesser developed countries, Japan's exports were capital-intensive and its imports labor-intensive. Since 75 percent of Japan's trade is with developing countries, the paradox for overall trade is explained. Thus, on a more refined basis, the Heckscher-Ohlin theorem appears to hold for Japan.

India. A study by Bharadwaj (1962) found that India tends to export labor-intensive goods and import capital-intensive goods. Thus it appears that the Heckscher-Ohlin model applies to India. However, when the bilateral trade of India with the United States was examined, it was found that India exports capital-intensive goods but imports labor-intensive goods. Thus, at a very disaggregated level, the Heckscher-Ohlin model appears not to hold. Notice that the aggregate-disaggregate Heckscher-Ohlin results for India are exactly the reverse of those for Japan.

East Germany. Stolper and Rosekamp (1961) examined East Germany's trade. By comparison with the rest of Eastern Europe, East Germany is capital abundant. Using input-output techniques, these authors found that in fact East Germany exported capital-intensive goods and imported labor-intensive goods from its eastern European bloc trading partners. (They account for three-fourths of East Germany's trade.)

Canada. Wahl (1961) found that the capital-labor ratio for Canadian exports exceeded that for the Canadian import-competing production. Most of Canada's trade is with the United States; this is consistent with Leontief's finding for the United States.

What can cause the Heckscher-Ohlin predictions to fail? The results above show a rather mixed pattern in the ability of the theorem to predict trade flows. While there are many factors that can cause the assumptions of a theorem to fail and hence its predictions to be inaccurate, we can cite at least four important considerations.

First, the Heckscher-Ohlin theorem is a *supply-oriented* model. It assumes that the consumers' preference for cars to trucks is the same between economies, and that a country's exports can be predicted by the factor intensities of the product and the factor endowments of the countries. However, it is clear that different preferences in two countries can cause the trade pattern to go the other way. Thus, even though the United States might have a comparative production advantage in capital-intensive goods, if U.S. citizens had strong preferences for capital-intensive goods and foreign consumers preferred labor-intensive goods, then the Leontief paradox could be explained. That is, the U.S. comparative production advantage in capital-intensive goods would be more than offset by the desire of Americans to consume them so that capital-intensive goods would be imported into the United States to satisfy total demand. The evidence on this question is quite mixed. Houthakker (1957) found that the income elasticities of demand for a wide variety of products are fairly similar across countries. Thus it should not be true that low-income countries would have a stronger preference, say, for clothing than the United States. Other evidence is available, however, from Vernon's product cycle, which will be studied in Chapter 3. The United States tends to be the first country in the world to consume very sophisticated consumer products, so that it has very strong demands for the types of products in which it has a comparative advantage in production. Thus the question of how tastes affect trade flows is an open one.

Second, any economic condition that can *reverse the pattern of trade* will cause the Heckscher-Ohlin predictions to be reversed. For example, if a labor union or any factor of production causes the export industry to pay more for a factor than import-competing industries do, then the export industry will contract. If it contracts far enough, the good that used to be exported may become the importable. Thus, even though the United States may be relatively well endowed with capital, it would have to import capital-intensive goods if labor unions or other distortions in factor markets caused U.S. production of these goods to fall sufficiently.

Third, some products will be capital-intensive at very high prices of capital and labor-intensive at very low relative prices of capital. This phenomenon is known as a *factor-intensity reversal.* Minhas (1962) found that factor reversals occurred in 15 out of 24 industries. Since it might be possible for automobiles to be capital intensive in the United States, but for them to be relatively labor intensive at a different factor price structure in Japan, then it is difficult to tell whether the Heckscher-Ohlin theorem will work. Another assumption of the Heckscher-Ohlin model is that the technology used to combine capital and labor for production in the United States is the same technology available worldwide. If this assumption is also violated, then it is hard to tell whether the model will have much predictive power. Minhas, in fact, found a low correlation between capital and labor ratios in 20 industries in the United States and the same labor-capital ratios in Japan.

Fourth, while *tariffs* do not reverse the pattern of trade, they could generate a result similar to Leontief's. Taxing a good that is imported cannot make it an exportable. If the tariff becomes prohibitively high, the United States will simply fail to import the good. At the high U.S. price, no U.S. producer would want to sell it abroad at the lower world price. However, if it is true that tariffs are weighted toward discouraging imports of labor-intensive products, then any test of the factor intensities of U.S. trade could be biased. (Evidence showing that effective tariffs tend to be high on low-wage industries will be presented in Chapter 5.) Thus labor-intensive imports are greatly underrepresented in observed U.S. imports because of the high tariff on them.

However, an important consideration is that the simple two factor (capital-labor) model still does not capture all of the factors of production. We turn now to a discussion of the importance of both natural resources and human capital.

Other Factors of Production

Compared with the rest of the world, it appears that the United States is poorly endowed with natural resources relative to other factors. Vanek

(1959) found that U.S. exports embodied only about half of the natural resources contained in U.S. imports. Thus the United States appears to be importing resources as a scarce factor of production. This observation is consistent with the Heckscher-Ohlin theorem.

A more important consideration is the failure to adjust for human capital. Relative to other countries, the United States has its greatest abundance of human capital in the form of education. A capital good is defined as a durable asset, and education certainly qualifies as a durable asset, albeit intangible. Vernon's product cycle suggests that the United States is exploiting its comparative abundance of skilled labor. Data by Gruber, Mehta, and Vernon (1967) showed that U.S. export industries tend to use highly skilled labor. Thus when this consideration is incorporated, it appears that the United States may conform to the theory in exporting skilled labor-intensive products and in importing unskilled labor products. In effect, it is economizing on its scarce factor of imports and exploiting its comparative advantage in skilled labor through its exports.

2.3   OTHER THEORIES OF COMPARATIVE ADVANTAGE

Scale Economies

Hufbauer (1970) has suggested that large countries will export products requiring relatively large plant sizes and small countries will specialize in the production of products in which the optimum plant size is small. Although the correlation between the size of an economy and the importance of scale economies in production of exports was high, it was not statistically significant. However, when Hufbauer correlated the GNP per capita with scale economies of exports, he found an extremely strong fit. Thus it appears that the ability of an economy to mass-produce goods is even more closely related to the degree of sophistication of the economy than with the absolute size of its industrial sector. Further evidence of this phenomenon has been reported by Grubel (1977, p. 80), who found that before European economic integration, European plants tended to have higher costs than U.S. plants because European plants were producing more varieties, styles, and sizes of the same commodity than did the corresponding U.S. plant. Thus it is not just the size of the plant that is important in measuring scale economies; at least as important is the length of run. These runs tended to be long in the United States, but short in Europe.

Demand Similarities

Nearly all of the aforementioned theories have focused on various characteristics of either production or supply. Linder (1961) suggested a demand-based theory of comparative advantage. He speculated that countries tend to produce and export the quality of product demanded by most of the people within its borders, while it imports products that are geared primarily to minorities, either the very rich or the very poor. The empirical implication of this theory is that countries with fairly similar levels of per capita income will tend to trade with each other since they will both produce goods that are appropriate for the income level of the average citizen in their countries.

In an empirical test of a number of theories of comparative advantage, Hufbauer (1970) found that a country's imports tend to embody characteristics that are exactly the reverse of its exports. His results provide indirect evidence that countries basically engage in trade in order to compensate for national deficiencies. This is consistent with the orthodox theories of Ricardo, Heckscher-Ohlin, and scale economies. Basically the *compensation approach* suggests that if an economy tends to export highly capital-intensive goods, it will import highly labor-intensive goods; if it exports goods employing large amounts of skilled labor, it will import goods using primarily unskilled labor; if it exports goods utilizing large economies of scale, it will import goods that are not primarily based on economies of scale. This is in contrast with the Linder (1961) theory, which suggests that countries import the same types of goods that they export, namely, those that satisfy the average citizen in the economy.

In this chapter we have explored the classic theory of comparative advantage and empirical tests of it. The basic message is that there are gains to be had from production specialization. The story of Marco Polo provides an example of this principle. He spent over 30 years in the Far East with his father and uncle collecting information about a civilization which was largely unknown to Europe. He returned to Venice in 1292 but was captured in a naval battle between Venice and Genoa in 1295. His stories of the marvels of the East would not have been preserved had he not spent two years in a jail in Genoa. There he told and retold the stories of his travels. However, Marco Polo did not commit these to paper; rather, they were written by a fellow prisoner, Rusticello. Thus, Marco Polo and Rusticello used the theory of comparative advantage: Marco Polo had the stories, Rusticello had the writing ability and together they created a best seller.

There are also historical examples of failure to appreciate the theory of comparative advantage. For example, Greenberg (1951) quotes an emperor of China who is reported to have said that China did not need to trade with Europe because "We possess all things."

REFERENCES

1. Bharadwaj, R., "Factor Proportions and the Structure of Indo-U.S. Trade," *Indian Economic Journal* **10** (October 1962): 105–116.
2. Grubel, Hubert G., *International Economics*. Homewood, Illinois: Richard D. Irwin, 1977, Chs. 2, 3, and 4.
3. Gruber, W., Mehta, D., and Vernon, R., "The R & D Factor in International Trade and International Investment of the United States Industries," *Journal of Political Economy* **75** (February 1967): 20–37.
4. Hart, E.H., *Marco Polo*. Norman, Oklahoma: University of Oklahoma Press, 1967.
5. Houthakker, H.S., "An International Comparison of Household Expenditure Patterns, Commemorating the Centenary of Engel's Law," *Econometrica* **25** (October 1957): 532–551.
6. Hufbauer, G.C., "The Impact of National Characteristics and Technology on the Commodity Composition of Trade in Manufactured Goods," in R. Vernon, ed., *The Technology Factor in International Trade*. New York: Columbia University Press, 1970: 145–231.
7. Ichimura, S. and Tatemoto, M., "Factor Proportions and Foreign Trade: The Case of Japan," *Review of Economics and Statistics* **41** (November 1959): 442–446.
8. Leontief, W.W., "Domestic Production in Foreign Trade: The American Capital Position Re-examined," *Economia Internazionale* **7** (February 1954): 9–38.
9. Linder, Staffan B., *An Essay on Trade and Transformation*. New York: John Wiley & Sons, 1961.
10. MacDougall, D., "British and American Exports: A Study Suggested by the Theory of Comparative Cost," *Economic Journal* **61** (December 1951): 697–724.
11. Minhas, B., "The Homohyphallagic Production Function, Factor-Intensity Reversals, and the Heckscher-Ohlin Theorem," *Journal of Politcal Economy* **70** (April 1962): 138–156.
12. Stolper, W. and Rosekamp, K.W., "An Input-Output Table for East Germany with Applications to Foreign Trade," *Oxford University. Institute of Economics and Statistics Bulletin* **23** (November 1961): 379–392.
13. Vanek, J., "The Natural Resource Content of Foreign Trade, 1870–1955, and the Relative Abundance of Natural Resources in the United States," *Review of Economics and Statistics* **41** (May 1959): 146–153.
14. Wahl, D.F., "Capital and Labour Requirements for Canada's Foreign Trade," *Canadian Journal of Economics* **27** (August 1961): 349–358.

International 3
Trade in
New Products

This chapter is really about theories of the MNC.

New and exotic ideas have always been an important stimulus to international trade. When Marco Polo returned to Venice from the Far East in 1292, his tales about unfamiliar technologies possessed by the Chinese stimulated more interest in trade with the Far East than could have been generated by a century of students extolling the theory of comparative costs. Today, an important vehicle for the international transmission of new commercial ideas is the multinational corporation.

In 1970, 31 percent of U.S. exports were to majority-owned foreign affiliates of U.S.-based multinational corporations and 28 percent of U.S. imports were from majority-owned foreign affiliates of U.S.-based multinational corporations (U.S. Tariff Commission, 1963, p. 180). In this chapter we investigate five different theories about multinational corporations as agents of international trade in new products: the comparative advantage, imperfect competition, appropriability, product cycle, and capital market theories.

3.1 THE COMPARATIVE ADVANTAGE THEORY

The theories of comparative advantage investigated in Chapter 2 stress that countries export goods in which they possess some advantage in produc-

28

tion over foreign countries. The Heckscher-Ohlin theorem states that countries export goods that use a lot of the country's most abundant resources. In the case of high-technology goods, the theorem means that countries with skilled-labor forces will export high-technology products, while those with unskilled-labor forces will export low-technology (or standardized) products. Thus we should observe the United States and other developed countries exporting sophisticated consumer and producer goods, and the developing countries exporting less sophisticated products. Since this is the case, the theory squares with the stylized facts.

3.2 IMPERFECT COMPETITION (Hymer)

Multinational corporations have disadvantages compared with local firms in many countries. They have all the disadvantages of any outsider: They are in a hostile political, economic, cultural, language, legal, and social environment. They can operate successfully only if they have an economic advantage over local firms. Hymer (1960) suggests that this advantage is superior technology and management abilities. Multinational corporations usually succeed only if they have a new product that local firms cannot supply, because the local firms do not possess necessary technology, or if they can produce standardized goods using a more sophisticated production technology than is available to local producers.

Caves (1971) extended this hypothesis by suggesting that high-technology products tend to be transmitted abroad along industry lines. He called this *horizontal direct investment,* which is to be contrasted with *vertical direct investment* whereby firms organize internationally and locate different stages of production in different countries. (Other hypotheses will be considered at length in the discussion of raw materials in Chapter 4.) Hymer and Caves also noted that high technology industries tend to be concentrated and to be characterized by oligopolistic structures, meaning that there are only a few producers. Furthermore, the noncompetitive industry structure that exists at home tends to be replicated when the same industry produces abroad. For example, the U.S. automobile industry is characterized by three giants: General Motors, Ford, and Chrysler. In many foreign automobile markets, the same three firms also appear.

A third characteristic of the imperfect competition model is that since an oligopolistic structure exists, much nonprice competition occurs: Rather than competing excess profits to zero, firms in an oligopolistic industry compete on the basis of advertising, service, and other nonprice variables. Examples of industries in which much horizontal direct investment occurs (which also happen to be concentrated) include those that produce automobiles, other consumer durables, scientific instruments, chemicals, and rubber.

3.3 APPROPRIABILITY (Magee)

Thomas Edison spent more on legal fees attempting to protect the returns from his light bulb than he received in fees and royalties from that invention. This same sort of thing happens to innovating multinationals. The need to protect the returns from their innovations causes multinationals to behave in ways which have been explained by Magee (6) in his appropriability theory.

The appropriability theory suggests that the most important consideration facing innovating multinationals is the possible loss of the technology to rivals and copiers. New ideas are public goods, which means that anyone who can figure out how to use them may do so without reducing the use by others. But unauthorized use of new ideas certainly reduces the profitability for innovators. The conflict between the social use of the good and the private returns to the innovator has been termed the *appropriability problem.* When applied to the multinational corporation, the appropriability theory suggests that it is more efficient to transfer high technology worldwide inside firms than through the market because there is less likelihood of it being copied and stolen by outsiders if it is under the control of a single firm. An innovating firm will invest resources to keep others from copying and stealing the idea. The appropriability theory suggests that mechanisms evolve to prevent the loss of high technology and that these form a central theme that can explain much multinational corporation behavior.

It will explain, for example, why multinational corporations create very sophisticated technologies rather than simple ones. Sophisticated ideas are hard to copy while simple ideas are easy to copy. Therefore the appropriability problem is particularly severe for simple ideas. One implication of this hypothesis is that multinational corporations cannot be counted on to create the types of technology that are most useful for the developing countries. The developing countries need two types of technologies: simple production processes and simple products. However, the ability of private firms to capture the returns on these types of ideas is difficult. Production processes that use much unskilled labor tend to be either assembly-line operations for which multinationals can appropriate returns or so simple that research of the most efficient way to arrange unskilled laborers cannot yield a high return to the innovator because any improvement is easy to copy. The same is true for very simple goods: It is much easier for a copier to emulate the hula hoop than to discover the innovative components in an electronic computer.

We shall consider shortly the Vernon product cycle, which relates production location and product age. The appropriability theory suggests that the speed of product aging in the Vernon cycle is related to the industry technology cycle, developed by Magee (7); a listing of industries by age is provided in Table 3.1. So long as the innovating firms in an industry maintain their technological lead over emulating firms, the industry will remain young and produce new products. When appropriability mechanisms break down (e.g., industry structure becomes less concentrated), emulators in the U.S. and abroad reduce the profitability of innovation so that the industry's product line shifts to older, more standardized products.

The profit-maximizing strategy which innovating multinations will pursue in pricing their products in the face of eroding appropriability is explored by Magee (8). Even if the multinational is the only producer early in a product's life, it should sell below the monopoly price (since the monopoly price encourages emulator production which reduces the present value of future profits more than recouped by today's profits) and slowly cut the price as appropriability erodes until it hits the perfectly competitive level. The multinational's product market share hits zero just as the product becomes completely standardized. If the market share is still positive with standardization, the multinational has pursued too low a price strategy (i.e., discouraged emulators more than was in its own profit interests).

3.4   THE VERNON PRODUCT CYCLE

Vernon (1966) suggests that new products go through a life cycle of three stages: new product, maturing product, and standardized product. In Chapter 2 the theories of comparative advantage, which apply to international trade in standardized products, were discussed. In this chapter we focus on the more dynamic theories and emphasize their predictive ability for new products. Vernon observes that new products tend to be consumed and produced first in the United States and other high income countries. As they mature, the production location spreads to other developed countries. When they become standardized, production shifts into developing and low-wage countries.

Research Intensity

The amount of research and development needed to produce a sophisticated new product is high. Because of the comparative abundance of

Table 3.1 Average age of 36 industries in 1967

Less than 20 years		20 to 30 years		Over 30 years	
Sic No.	Name	Sic No.	Name	Sic No.	Name
2833	Medical Chemicals & Botanical products	2256	Knit Fabric Mills	2371	Fur goods
2834	Pharmaceutical Preparations	2335	Women's Dresses	3111	Leather Tanning & Finishing
3811	Engineering & Scientific & Research Instruments	2396	Automotive Fabric Trimmings & Apparel findings	3141	Shoes (Non-rubber)
3831	Optical Instruments & Lenses	2819	Miscellaneous Industrial Inorganic Chemicals	3161	Luggage
3841	Surgical & Medical Instruments	2861	Gum & wood chemicals	3171	Handbags & Purses
3843	Dental Equipment & Supplies	2891	Adhesives & chemicals	3241	Cement, hydraulic
3851	Ophthalmic Goods	3291	Abrasive Products	3274	Lime
3534	Elevators & Escalators	3293	Gaskets & Insulations	3281	Cut Stone & Stone Products
3536	Hoist, cranes & monorails	3312	Blast Furnaces & Steel Mills		
3541	Metal-cutting machine tools	3441	Fabricated Structural Steel		
3651	Radio & TV sets	3623	Electric Welding Apparatus		
3674	Semiconductors, etc.	3953	Marking Devices		
3861	Photographic equipment	2241	Narrow Fabric Mills		
		3322	Malleable Iron Foundaries		
		3552	Textile Machinery		

Source: Magee (1977, p. 311)

skilled labor in the United States it is logical that many such products would be developed there. As the product matures, the amount of ongoing research needed for the product diminishes. When the product gets to the third stage, little research is needed for its production: examples include textiles, bicycles, luggage, and cut stones.

Nature of the Product

New products tend to be highly differentiated. For example, early in this century, a wide variety of automobiles were produced by several dozen companies in the United States. The mass consumption of model A's and model T's signaled the move to a more standardized product. Because the form of the product changes rapidly, it is important that there be continuous interaction between consumers of the product and its producers. This is so that producers can get the "bugs" out of new models. When the product becomes older and standardized, it is by definition more homogeneous than when it was first developed and there is less pressure for production to be geographically close to the market.

Production Techniques

Production methods for new products tend to be less capital intensive than for older products. The reason is that the constant change in the nature of the product prohibits large-scale capital investments since production runs are short. As a result, the capital-labor ratio for new products tends to be lower than for the same product after it becomes standardized. Standardized products can be more easily produced by assembly line and mass-production techniques.

Product Demand

Demand considerations furnish two important reasons for the fact that new products are frequently developed in the United States. First, there is a demand for sophisticated capital equipment because of high unit labor costs in the United States. Producers are continually looking for a machine that will replace unskilled labor, a scarce factor in the United States whose price is sustained by labor unions, minimum wage laws, social security taxes, etc. Second, because the United States is at very high income levels, sophisticated consumers desire exotic new consumer goods as well as new household appliances to economize on time and the cost of household labor. This generates a greater demand for new products in high-income countries than in low-income countries. As incomes rise in other developed countries, consumers in those countries begin to use products that were produced earlier in the United States. Finally, when the product becomes standardized and incomes rise, it is eventually purchased in the developing countries.

Location of Production

Because of both supply and demand considerations, new products tend to be produced only in the United States or other countries of origin initially. The need for swift interaction between producers and consumers and some economies of scale in the United States dictate this location of production in stage I. In stage II, Western Europe and other developed countries erect tariff barriers on imports of these goods from the United States to encourage production in their countries. This, coupled with the increasing competitiveness of production of these products, makes more careful calculations of cost (transportation, tariffs, and other considerations) move U.S. production into lower-cost countries (other developed countries). Finally, when the production process is standardized and patents lapse on the original ideas, production moves to the low-cost world producers. Low-wage trade becomes important for standardized products and, to the extent that labor costs are still important, some products will be produced in the developing countries.

International Trade

It should be clear from the above discussion that the United States is the prime producer of many new products and exports these goods to other developed economies in stage I. In stage II, production in other developed economies starts to displace imports from the U.S. and replaces U.S. exports to the developing countries. In stage III the production moves into developing countries and the goods are exported back to the United States and other developed countries.

International Subcontracting

American multinational corporations have been able to short circuit some of the long time periods in the Vernon product cycle through international subcontracting. The strategy has been for the American multinationals to assemble those very labor-intensive portions of high-technology goods in developing countries. This possibility was made profitable by items 806.30 and 807.00 of the U.S. Tariff Schedules, whereby import duties on items coming into the United States would be levied only on the amount of value generated abroad if the original inputs originated in the United States. For example, if electronic components worth $5 are exported from the United States to Taiwan and assembled into an electronic calculator worth $8, when the calculator is imported into the United States, a duty is paid only on the $3 that was generated abroad. Imports of this type from developing countries to the United States have risen from $61 million in 1966 to $539 million in 1970 to $1.4 billion in 1973 (Morrison, 1976, p. 33).

Furthermore, the share of U.S. subcontracted imports in total U.S. manufactured imports from the developing countries rose from 6.4 percent in 1966 to 22 percent in 1972.

The following table shows the share of imports from the developing countries that entered under tariff item 807.00 in 1969.

U.S. imports from developing countries
under tariff item 807.00, 1969

Product	Percentage
Textile products	8.6
Office machines	8.3
TV receivers	10.8
TV apparatus	8.3
Semiconductors	23.6
Electronic memories	10.2
Toys, dolls	5.9

Source: U.S. Tariff Commission, Economic Factors Affecting the Use of the Items 807.00 and 806.30 of the Tariff Schedules of the United States, (Washington, D.C., 1970) and Morrison (1976, p. 34).

The importance of subcontracting in this type of trade is related to the amount of unskilled labor required for assembly and the wages abroad. The multinationals are strongly motivated to subcontract to the developing countries since their unit labor costs are only 27 percent of unit labor costs in the United States. There is also considerable variation around this average, which ranges from 7 percent for baseballs to 46 percent for scientific instruments. Furthermore, this subcontracting frequently is not in the more wealthy developing countries but in the poorer developing countries. For example, Haiti is listed by the United Nations as one of the 25 "least developed countries" but through this provision of the U.S. Tariff Code, it provides nearly half of the U.S. imports of baseballs.

Examples

Stage I products include large computer systems, jet aircraft, medical equipment, space technology, and atomic reactors. More mature stage II products include automobiles, motorcycles, desk calculators, medium-size computers, and many types of steel. Standardized products include bicycles, textiles, simple electronic components, and piece goods.

The evidence in Table 3.2 from Gruber, Mehta, and Vernon (1967) shows the importance of research and development in U.S. exports. Notice

Table 3.2   Research effort and world trade performance by U.S. industries, 1962

	5 industries with highest research effort	14 other industries	All 19 industries
Research effort			
Total R&D expenditures as percentage of sales	6.3	0.5	2.0
Scientists and engineers in R&D as percentage of total employment	3.2	0.4	1.1
Export performance			
Exports as percentage of sales	7.2	1.8	3.2
Excess of exports over imports, as percentage of sales	5.2	-1.1	0.6

Source: W. H. Gruber, Dileep Mehta, and Raymond Vernon (1967).

that industries with a high percentage of scientists and engineers engaged in research and development as a percentage of the total industry employment also tend to have a large trade balance (excess of exports over imports) as a percentage of industry sales: chemicals, electrical machinery, transportation, and instruments. In five out of the 19 industries with the highest research effort, the trade balance as a percentage of sales is 5.2 percent, while all other industries have negative trade balances.

3.5   THE CAPITAL MARKET THEORY (Aliber)

Aliber (1970) observed that monopolistic advantage over new technology or superior organization may be an important consideration in the explanation of multinational corporation behavior. However, he points out that real considerations dictate where products will be produced in the world (these include all of the four theories above plus other variables such as wages, taxes, tariffs, etc.), but that capital market considerations are important in explaining who owns these operations. For example, if the rates of return on investments are 8 percent in the United States and 12 percent in Western Europe, then U.S. investors would go to Western Europe and purchase their securities and factories. This process would continue until risk-adjusted rates of return are pushed together.

This theory provides one explanation of how U.S. multinational corporations took over Europe (see Servan-Schreiber). If a project has an expected return of 10 percent in Western Europe (and discount rates are 8 percent in the U.S. and 12 percent in Europe), then a U.S. multinational is more likely to undertake this project since it would earn a higher rate of return than could be obtained at home. But a Western European firm would not undertake this project since it earns less than the cost of capital in Europe. Since Western European capital markets were notoriously imperfect until sometime in the 1960s, this is one explanation of the rapid expansion of multinationals in Western Europe and the rest of the world.

example

It should be pointed out that some type of <u>market segmentation is needed for this theory</u> to explain direct investment and multinational corporation expansion. It should be true that rates of return will be driven together as investments leave countries with low rates of return and are invested in countries with high rates of return. <u>Aliber's explanation of long-period U.S. direct investment is that currencies such as the dollar have a "premium" on them.</u> Consider an extreme case. If everyone in the world wants to keep his investments in the United States, then the rate of return on investments in the United States will be below those in the rest of the world. Why, then, does there exist a premium on the dollar? This is difficult to explain. However, Aliber claims that because of <u>less political risk</u> in the United States (less threat of expropriation and loss of securities because of government caprice) and <u>more efficient institutions</u> matching borrowers and lenders, a permanent premium may exist on the dollar.

permanent premium on US $.

REFERENCES

1. Aliber, Robert Z., "The Theory of the International Corporation: A Theory of Direct Foreign Investment," in Kindleberger, C.P., *The International Corporation*. Cambridge, Mass.: MIT Press, 1970: 17–34.

2. Caves, Richard E., "International Corporations: The Industrial Economics of Foreign Investment," *Economica, N.S.* **38** (February 1971): 1–27

3. Coase, Ronald H., "The Nature of the Firm," *Economica, N.S.* **4** (November 1937): 386–405.

4. Gruber, W., Mehta, D., and Vernon, R., "The R & D Factor in International Trade and International Investment of the United States Industries." *Journal of Political Economy* **75** (February 1967): 20–37.

5. Hymer, Stephen H., *The International Operations of National Firms: A Study of Direct Foreign Investment*. Cambridge, Mass.: MIT Press, 1976 (originally presented as the author's thesis, MIT, 1960).

6. Magee, Stephen P., "Information and the Multinational Corporation: An Appropriability Theory of Direct Foreign Investment," in Bhagwati, J., ed., *The New International Economic Order: The North-South Debate*. Cambridge, Mass.: MIT Press, 1977: 317–340.

7. ———, "Multinational Corporations, The Industry Technology Cycle and Development," *Journal of World Trade Law* **11** (July/August 1977): 279–321.

8. ———, "Application of the Dynamic Limit Pricing Model to the Price of Technology and International Technology Transfer," in Brunner, Karl and Meltzer, Allan H., eds., *Optimal Policies, Control Theory and Technology of Exports.* Amsterdam: North-Holland, 1977: 203–224.

9. Morrison, Thomas K., *Manufactured Exports for Developing Countries.* New York: Praeger, 1976.

10. Schumpeter, J.A., *Capitalism, Socialism and Democracy.* 3rd Edition. New York: Harper and Row, 1950, Chapters VII and VIII.

11. Servan-Schreiber, J.J., *The American Challenge.* New York: Avon Books, 1967.

12. United States Tariff Commission, *Implications of Multinational Firms for World Trade and Investment and for U.S. Trade and Labor.* A Study for the Committee on Finance, United States Senate, 93rd Congress, 1st Session, February, 1973, Washington: U.S. Government Printing Office.

13. Vernon, Raymond, "International Investment and International Trade in the Product Cycle," *Quarterly Journal of Economics* **80** (May 1966): 190–207.

A

We will appreciate

YOUR ACKNOWLEDGMENT OF THE RECEIPT
OF THIS BOOK AND YOUR OPINION OF IT.

Simply detach the card.

It is mailable without postage.

Thank you.

**ADDISON-WESLEY
PUBLISHING COMPANY, INC.**

THE COPY OF _____ HAS BEEN RECEIVED

(Please fill in title and author of book here)

MY OPINION OF THIS BOOK IS: _____ DATE _____

_____

(Please check here if we may quote you in our advertising ☐)

Author of text now in use _____ Class Enrollment _____

Professor in charge of course _____ Course Name _____

Do you expect to adopt this book? _____ When? _____

NAME _____ TITLE _____ DEPT. _____

SCHOOL _____

CITY _____ STATE _____ ZIP _____

Telephone _____ Office Hours _____

Please detach this stub before mailing

WILL YOU KINDLY FILL IN AND MAIL THE ATTACHED CARD? NO POSTAGE IS REQUIRED. WE SHALL GREATLY APPRECIATE HAVING YOUR OPINION OF THIS BOOK.

Course name information will help us correct our records. Name of professor in charge of course, if other than yourself, will permit sending new information or supplementary material, such as answer books, errata sheets, new problems, etc., to the proper persons.

Thank you.

ADDISON-WESLEY PUBLISHING COMPANY, INC.

International 4
Trade in
Raw
Materials

[handwritten notes:]
Magee & Robbins (1978),
Raw Material Product Cycle.

Case Studies:
1. Rubber
2. Industrial diamonds
3. Tin

Because of the uneven distribution of minerals in the earth's crust, international trade is important for raw materials markets. Industrialization and decreasing transportation costs have provided an important stimulus to international trade in raw materials. On the other hand, international trade in raw materials has been discouraged by the development of synthetics and reductions in the use of primary raw materials brought about through research and development. The net effect of these forces appears to be favorable to raw materials and food exporters over the last century and a half. Notice in Table 4.1 that these commodities have dropped dramatically as U.S. exports and risen as U.S. imports since 1820. In Section 4.1, we investigate long-term cycles in raw materials trade. Section 4.2 addresses the question of whether we are going to run out of raw materials. Section 4.3 considers the extent to which research and development provides a substitute for international trade in raw materials. Section 4.4 examines international commodity agreements.

There are several important economic characteristics of trade in raw materials. The first is that the elasticity of demand for raw materials both in domestic consumption and in international trade appears to be inelastic. This means that if the price rises by 1 percent, there is a less than 1 percent reduction in the quantity of the raw material consumed. The most widely accepted explanation for this phenomenon is that raw materials are a

39

Table 4.1   Crude materials and food stuffs as a percentage of total U.S. international trade, 1820–1959

Year	As a percentage of exports	As a percentage of imports
1820	65	16
1850	68	18
1861–70	54	26
1881–90	54	37
1901–10	42	46
1921–25	37	49
1926–30	31	49
1936–40	23	46
1946–50	22	49
1956–59	20	38

Source: Kindleberger (1962, p. 41).

"derived demand." Many raw materials are inputs into the production of final products. For example, rubber might be price inelastic for automobile manufacturers because rubber must be used in tires for automobiles. If the price of rubber rises, automobile companies are not likely to reduce the number of tires from four to three. While there can be minor economies in the use of rubber for automobile tires in the short run, automobile manufacturers will continue to purchase the same number and size of tires. Thus, inelastic demand is a common characteristic of many types of raw materials. Consequently, as the supply of a raw material varies, its price is going to exhibit more substantial fluctuations than the quantity of the raw material consumed.

One implication of inelastic demand is that producers would have an economic incentive to reduce the quantity supplied in order to raise the world price. We shall explore various attempts by raw materials and commodity exporters to raise the world price through commodity agreements in Section 4.4.

Although the demands for raw materials may be inelastic in the short run, the demand is much higher over long periods of time. In order to economize on the use of high priced raw materials, research and development and modified behavior by consumers is required. While these actions may take some period of time to produce results, they are nevertheless a very powerful force. We turn now to a description of some of the pressures that are exerted over long periods of time in raw materials markets.

4.1   A RAW MATERIAL CYCLE

We discovered in Chapter 3 that new products tend to have a life cycle. This life cycle starts with a research and development breakthrough in the developed countries. Production occurs in the developed countries for many years and then in its late life, it tends to move into developing countries.

Even though it is dangerous to generalize about raw materials, there is a noticeable tendency for exactly the reverse process to occur in the case of international trade raw materials. Many raw materials which are important for industrial activity in the West are located in developing countries. These countries are net exporters of raw materials to advanced industrial countries. However, there is a noticeable life cycle in certain raw materials and an observable tendency to be exactly the reverse of Vernon's cycle for manufactured products. Mainly, production of raw materials is very important in developing countries early in its "life," but the production of these raw materials gradually switches to the developed countries late in their life. The reason for this curious phenomenon is the development of synthetic alternatives to the raw material, which can be produced in almost any world location. However, because synthetics require high technology, their production stays in the developed countries for long periods of time. It is important to emphasize that the "raw material" produced in the developed countries is not the same physical commodity as the primary raw material. For example, in the case of rubber, most of the world production was located in the developing countries at the beginning of this century. But, today over two-thirds of the world's rubber production is synthetic and many of the plants are located in advanced industrial countries. Another example is industrial diamonds. Through time, there has been a decreasing proportion of primary diamond production and an increasing share of synthetic diamond production. Again, since the latter is done largely in developed countries, there is a noticeable shift in the world production of the services provided for the combined primary and synthetic diamond. The single most important empirical evidence is the following: in 1960, 86 percent of synthetic materials were produced in six developed countries; a much smaller percent of primary raw material production occurs in these six countries.

A second implication of a life-cycle approach to raw materials trade is that technological breakthroughs determine both important increases in the demand for primary raw materials early in its life as well as declines in the demand for it late in the cycle. For example, each raw material that is important in international trade today had, at some point, an increase in the demand for it generated by some sort of technological breakthrough. For rubber, it was the development of the automobile; for tin it was the invention of automatic canning machinery; for industrial diamonds it was the development of cemented carbide cutting tools, which allowed the diamonds to be held for cutting purposes; for copper it was the development of electricity. All of these developments led to rapid increases in the price of the raw material. There is downward pressure on price later in the raw material's life as high-technology importing countries develop synthetic alternatives or sophisticated techniques for economizing on the use of the raw material. For rubber and industrial diamonds, it has been the development of synthetic alternatives; for tin, it was the shift to electrolytic plating procedures; for copper, it was the development of alternative conductors.

A third implication of the raw materials cycle is that eventual exhaustion of world supplies of the primary raw material does not mean that its services are lost. We may run short of primary diamonds but we will not run out of both primary and synthetic diamonds right away. In addition to recycling, reclamation, and substitution of a raw material that is rising in price, research and development extends the use of a raw material either by economizing on the dwindling supply through the use of new techniques or by developing synthetic alternatives, such as synthetic petroleum, which is now being developed from coal. Thus, while the world supply of a given primary raw material may dwindle, this usually does not mean that we will lose the services it provides.

A fourth implication is that the relative price of a raw material will be rising when it is in the first stage of the raw material cycle (when demand is increasing), while the terms of trade of the primary raw material will fall late in the cycle (when synthetics and other alternatives are coming on stream). For the first two-thirds of this century, the average price of raw materials has been remarkably constant relative to other goods. Thus while some raw materials have been in the up-phase of their cycle, others have been in the down-phase. One reason that the price of raw materials, relative to the price of manufactured goods, may not have changed is that any raw material in short supply will generate investment in research and development to economize on it. Eventually, a synthetic is developed or a technological breakthrough occurs, which allows consumers of raw materials to pay less for the same amount of primary raw materials. For example, when the price of petroleum is very high, private companies and governments in petroleum consuming countries spend large amounts on research and development to economize on oil. Later, if the relative price of oil falls sufficiently, this research and development may be channeled into another raw material in short supply, such as zinc or tin. Research and development continually shifts its focus from one raw material to another in an effort to adjust the market for an overpriced product.

A final implication of the raw materials cycle is that technological advance is a substitute for international trade in primary raw materials. During wars, international trade in all goods, including raw materials, is disrupted and the shortage of raw materials in consuming countries seriously hinders them unless they are able to develop alternatives. For example, during the Second World War the world's rubber source in the Far East was cut off from the West. Even though Germany had developed a synthetic rubber in World War I, the cutoff of the supply of primary rubber in World War II provided the incentive for both Germany and the United States to increase their efforts to develop a cheaper synthetic rubber. In fact, the Germans worked hard on the development of synthetic petroleum (developing gas fuels from coal) through the 1930s as a result of their shortage in World War I. By 1941, over one-third of German fuels were by synthesis from coal.

These implications were drawn from the histories of several raw materials. Their behavior has exhibited sufficient historical regularity to permit the description of a raw materials cycle. The cycle, developed by Magee and Robins (1978), has three stages.

    I. Derived Demand Boom
    II. Substitution in Demand and Supply Sources
    III. Synthetic and/or Research and Development Incursion.

3 stages of Raw Materials Cycle

In stage I there is a large increase in the demand for a product that uses the raw material in its production. This leads to a substantial increase in the price of the raw material. In stage II, the price increase is slowed down or the price of the raw material may actually fall as alternative world sources of supply for the primary raw material are opened up and users of the product replace it with cheaper alternatives. In stage III, research and development finally results in the development of either a synthetic alternative or an important way to economize on the use of the raw material. Let us consider case studies of three raw materials that fit the cycle; one is renewable, and two are nonrenewable raw materials. The first is a nonfood agricultural product, rubber; the second, a nonferrous metal, tin; and the third, a nonmetallic mineral, industrial diamonds.

Case

Rubber

The first stage for the rubber cycle lasted from about 1895 to about 1910. The new demand for rubber was derived from the development of the automobile, causing rubber prices to rise by 78 percent from 1900 to 1910. In the second stage, there was a shift from the traditional suppliers to other, more marginal suppliers of rubber. The second stage lasted from approximately 1910 to 1940. An interesting development is the extent to which the traditional suppliers lost their hold on the market: In 1910, Brazil and a few African countries supplied over 61 percent of world rubber production, but by 1930, Malaya, Ceylon (Sri Lanka), and Indonesia had 92 percent of the world rubber market. The shortage of rubber over this period resulted in substantial economies in its use. Initially tire life averaged only about 10,000 miles, but improved tire construction increased it to 20,000 miles and ultimately research and development permitted radial ply tires to last as many as 50,000 miles. Also, the proportion of raw rubber required per passenger mile was reduced significantly by adding oil, using reclaimed rubber, and recapping. During the period from 1910 to 1940, the price of rubber relative to other products fell substantially, while primary rubber consumption rose from 103 to 1128 metric tons. Finally, the third stage of the rubber cycle has lasted from approximately 1940 to the present. We have known how to synthesize rubber since the late 1800s but it was not until World War II that processes that made synthetic rubber a profitable substitute were developed. In 1955 the United States government released its synthetic rubber works to the private sector. Synthetic rubber was only about 20 percent of world rubber consumption in the 1940s; by 1962 it was 50 percent and by 1970 it was over 65 percent.

Industrial Diamonds

The first stage for the industrial diamonds raw material cycle was a period from 1930 to 1940. It was stimulated by the development of cemented carbide metal cutting tools: From 1936 to 1942 the use of these tools increased more than fifty-fold. The price of diamonds does not follow the raw material cycle exactly in stage 1 since there was not an increase in the price of diamonds in the 1930s. In fact, their price was falling because of the development in the late '20s and early '30s of increased diamond production capacity in the diamond-producing areas of Africa. From 1940 to 1960 we observed the second stage for industrial diamonds. Here there was increased exploration for alternative supplies and users substituted hard cutting materials as an alternative to diamonds. These included synthesized boron nitrate, which was developed by General Electric; ultrasonic abrasive grinding; and secondary recovery of diamonds, which was facilitated by electrostatic separation processes. These processes permitted firms to recover diamonds from old grinders, so that as many as two million karats a year were recovered in 1962 (approximately 10 percent of world production). The third stage of the diamond cycle has lasted from 1960 to the present. This was occasioned by the development of synthetic diamonds by General Electric in 1955. The process was the application of extremely high temperatures and pressure to pure carbon. The production of synthetic diamonds is now largely located in the developed countries; plants are operating in South Africa, Ireland, Japan, Sweden and the Soviet Union.

Tin

The first stage in the tin cycle lasted from 1895 to 1910. The surge in the demand for tin was stimulated by the invention of automatic can making machinery in 1895. As a result, tin prices rose by 144 percent from 1895 to 1910. Because of the high price of tin relative to other metals, cans were approximately 98 percent steel (or iron) and less then 2 percent tin. Tin is used to coat the can so that it will not rust like the ferrous metals. The substitution in demand and supply-switching stage lasted from approximately 1910 to 1945. In 1910, Malaysia, Singapore, the United Kingdom, and Indonesia supplied 95 percent of world tin. By the 1920s the share of these four countries had fallen to 70 percent of world production. By 1936, their share was 36 percent. Important new suppliers of tin became Bolivia, Thailand, and Australia. In the second stage, there was also increased secondary recovery of tin scrap: U.S. secondary consumption rose from 18 to 33 percent of total consumption from 1936 to 1945. There was increased use of alternative containers: glass, paper, aluminum, and plastics. The relative price of tin was virtually unchanged from 1910 to the 1940s, although world consumption of primary tin increased from 117,000 to 149,000 metric tons. The major research and development breakthrough that economized on the use of tin was not a synthetic alternative but an economy move. The R & D breakthrough was the development of the electroplating process. The old hot-dip process, by which steel cans were dipped into tin, resulted in cans containing 1.5 to 2.5 percent tin. The electroplating process is a procedure which requires that cans be placed in a room with ionized tin mist in the air and that an electrical charge be placed on them. Small amounts of tin adhere to the can through the field generated. This allows tin content as a percent of can weight to fall to one-quarter of 1 percent, a substantial saving.

The Synthetic Stage

An interesting aspect of the production of synthetics is that when a synthetic material begins to replace a primary raw material in stage III, the new synthetic product begins a Vernon life cycle of its own. Recall that with the Vernon life cycle, production begins in developed countries, slowly spreads to other developed countries, and finally ends up being produced in developing countries. In the case of synthetic rubber, we have evidence that this is the case (see Hufbauer, 1966, pp. 131–134). The first production date for synthetic rubber is shown in Table 4.2.

The Vernon-Hufbauer raw material synthetic cycle is generally faster than Vernon's product cycle for other advanced goods since production may move to the developing countries to economize on the cost of the raw

Table 4.2 Date of first production by country for styrene rubber

1941	United States
1943	Canada
1953	Germany*
1956	France
1957	Italy
1958	United Kingdom
1960	Japan
1960	Netherlands
1960	Brazil
1961	Australia
1965	Mexico

*Germany produced synthetic rubber before and during World War II but lost those plants to the Soviet Union at the end of the war.

material used for the synthetic (e.g., petrochemical production would move to OPEC countries faster than jet aircraft production). In fact, one puzzle is why production of synthetics does not move to its raw materials source more rapidly. Hufbauer reports that Canada was not a major exporter of viscose rayon in the 1960s despite large supplies of pulp wood. In the 19th century, Formosa and Japan were major suppliers of camphor, but Formosa never produced celluloid, the first plastic discovered that requires large amounts of camphor in its production, and Japan did not begin production until 1968, 40 years after the United States. Kuwait did not build a polyvinyl chloride plastic plant until 1963 (32 years after Germany), or a styrene rubber plant until 1965 (24 years after the United States), despite the fact that both of these synthetics are petroleum based. Hufbauer finds evidence that economies of scale in production which might be one reason for the slow dissemination from the original producing countries to the developing countries. Since large markets are important in the exploitation of economies of scale, large home markets are an important variable explaining synthetic exports in the postwar period. As in the case of manufactured products, the age of the synthetic is one of the best predictors of where the product will be produced. The older the product, the more likely it is to be produced in the developing countries.

4.2 SHORTAGES AND EXHAUSTIBLE RESOURCES: ARE WE GOING TO RUN OUT?

The raw material cycle emphasizes that there are many links between primary raw material sources and their ultimate uses in final products. Whenever a raw material shortage develops, these links can be constantly

[margin note: what should happen as we start "running out."]

adjusted so that the raw material in short supply has a rise in price resulting in (1) a cutback in their consumption; (2) a search for alternative sources of the same raw material or raw materials that substitute for it; (3) the discovery of new ways to economize on the raw material; (4) changes in production techniques; and (5) the development of synthetics. Pessimists argue that with the continued pressure of overpopulation and the limited supply of natural resources on this planet, we will eventually deplete our natural resources and face the specter of Malthusian starvation.

Optimists argue that the adjustment of markets and the ability to find substitutes for raw materials mean that society will continually adjust to any raw material that is in short supply. For example, the energy crisis is nothing new; there has been continual adjustment over the past century and a half to changing energy supplies. The energy crisis started in the mid-19th century. In 1850, wood supplied more than 90 percent of fuel-based energy in mineral fuels; in 1915, coal supplied 75 percent of energy requirements; and in 1970, petroleum and natural gas supplied over 80 percent.

[margin note: energy crisis began in 19th century!]

The same thesis applies to natural resources in general. Per capita consumption of natural resources, including agricultural products and timber, has increased only 55 percent in the past 100 years. Consumption of these items increased from $174 per capita in 1870 to $221 in 1900 and to $270 in 1954 (all in 1954 dollars). Our consumption of resources has also been continually declining as a share of total output: Output of resources as a percent of GNP has fallen from 36 percent in 1870 to 27 percent in 1900 to 12 percent in 1954. Thus, we have been adjusting to shortages for a long time.

4.3   RESEARCH AND DEVELOPMENT AS A SUBSTITUTE FOR TRADE

Traditional trade theory does not explain well the best response to temporary eliminations in international trade. It now appears, however, that research and development provides a major alternative to international trade. In wartime, there is a massive shortage in raw material-consuming countries in items that are important for manufacturing and for the war effort. As noted earlier, the reduction in the supply of rubber to the West in World War II following the Japanese capture of the Far East resulted in expanded research and development in synthetic rubber and its increased use. Liquid fuels were developed from coal, especially in Germany in World War II, and some plastic fibers were used extensively in order to economize on shortages of cotton. In World War I, Germany used synthetic rubber, viscose rayon, and glass filament fibers to counteract the blockade, which had reduced their imports of rubber, cotton, and asbestos.

Similarly, whenever war cuts off imports of manufactured goods into developing or agricultural economies, they reallocate and economize on the use of these products, increase their use of existing machines through greater repair and maintenance, and develop simple manufactured alternatives of their own.

It is an open question whether developed economies suffer more because of wartime severance from their raw material supplies, or whether the raw material suppliers suffer more because of their severance from manufactured goods. It would seem that developed economies, possessing greater human capital, would be better suited to adjusting to situations requiring innovation than underdeveloped economies. If this is the case, then the gains from trade are lower (or the loss from a severance in trade is less) in developed countries than in underdeveloped countries.

4.4   INTERNATIONAL COMMODITY AGREEMENTS

From time to time associations of either producers or producing countries attempt to affect international trade in primary commodities. During this century alone, there have been at least fifty attempts to control international commodity markets. There are two principal motivations for international commodity agreements: one is to raise the price of a commodity and the other is to moderate fluctuations in prices. One study indicates that for 19 out of 51 price-raising agreements (cartels), the agreement appears to have raised the prices of the commodity at least 200 percent above the unit costs of production and distribution. For example, OPEC successfully raised the price of petroleum over 400 percent in 1973 and 1974. Agreements aimed primarily at stabilizing prices are implemented by centralized holdings of buffer stocks. Whenever the price of a commodity is too high, sales are made from the buffer stock and when prices are too low, the buffer stock purchases the commodity. The object of this behavior is to stabilize the price beyond what it would be in the absence of the agreement.

Since both demand elasticities and supply elasticities tend to be low for many primary commodities, we might expect frequent fluctuations in price. For example, wide fluctuations in supply caused by weather conditions in growing countries will cause the price of foodstuffs and other commodities with low consumer responsiveness of quantity to price to fluctuate widely. Table 4.3 shows how the value, price, and quantity of a number of primary commodities varied in the period from 1948 to 1957. Notice that the highest fluctuations in the values of trade occurred in rubber, barley, jute, and copra. Very low fluctuations existed for sugar, tobacco, petroleum, and bananas. One interesting statistic is the correla-

Table 4.3 Short-period percentage fluctuations in world primary-commodity trade, 1948–1957

Commodity	Value	Price	Quantity
Natural rubber	30	25	7
Barley	25	15	14
Jute	21	16	16
Copra	19	16	10
Silk	18	9	19
Cocoa	17	19	7
Zinc	17	18	9
Wool	17	17	10
Coconut oil	17	17	10
Lead	16	18	14
Copper	15	15	6
Maize	15	13	10
Wheat	15	8	12
Cotton	14	13	8
Tin	14	10	15
Mutton and lamb	14	7	10
Rice	12	11	8
Tea	12	9	11
Aluminum	12	6	9
Beef and Veal	10	8	13
Butter	10	7	10
Cheese	10	7	7
Coffee	9	11	7
Sugar	6	6	4
Tobacco	6	4	6
Crude petroleum	4	5	3
Bananas	4	2	4
Means	14.0	11.6	9.6

Correlations:	Value	Price	Quantity
Value	1.00	—	—
Price	.84	1.00	—
Quantity	.50	.21	1.00

Source: MacBean (1966, p. 42). The short-period fluctuations are defined as the average annual absolute percentage deviation of trade from a five-year moving average.

tion between the value of trade and the price and quantity of trade. The correlations at the bottom of Table 4.3 indicate that the value of trade is more highly correlated with price than with quantity. Thus it appears that price is one of the more important determinants of export fluctuations for the commodities in the table.

What has been the history of international commodity agreements? Rowe (1965) has studied a number of international commodity agreements in the interwar period as well as in the 1950s. Many of the commodity agreements made in the 1920s collapsed or were broken up by the world depression in the 1930s. Commodity agreements made in the 1930s tended to come apart at the outbreak of World War II. For example, in 1926 a group of copper exporters formed an association to raise the price. The price rose well until there was a buyer's strike in March 1929, at which time the price dropped. Again in the late '30s, there was an attempt to raise the price through controls on production. However, several copper-producing regions refused to join the agreement (Canada, Europe, the Soviet Union, and Japan). This agreement ended with the outbreak of World War II.

An international rubber agreement lasted from 1922 to 1928. One mechanism by which the price of rubber was raised was the British compulsory restrictions placed on output in Malaya and Ceylon in 1922. Another rubber agreement, initiated in April 1934, was caused by surplus stocks and low prices of rubber. The price rose until the end of 1937, at which time the American recession caused a decrease in price.

Between 1933 and 1934, an agreement was reached between nine exporters and thirteen importers for wheat, but very little was accomplished in this agreement because Argentina breached its export quota. Quotas are usually placed on suppliers in order to hold down quantity and increase market price. However, in 1934 both the U.S. and Canadian crops were small, leading to price increases which made the agreement unnecessary.

An international agreement was reached in 1920 for trade in tea. However, unlike the terms of the wheat agreement most of the quantity restrictions were voluntary. Prices rose in that year simply because of bad weather and an increase in demand. Between April 1933 and late 1939 another international tea agreement was initiated. Typically, quotas by supplying countries were tightened in years of falling prices and relaxed in years of rising prices. The sugar agreements of the 1930s followed a similar pattern: Through Cuban initiation, production was limited to domestic consumption plus export quotas. While there was no direct price control, exports were controlled by quota and stocks were restricted. Again, in the 1950s, low prices induced formation of the International Sugar Agreement. Export quotas were imposed and prices remained high.

It is difficult to tell whether international commodity agreements aimed at *price* stabilization have been successful. Behrman (1978, p. 63) reviews very mixed results for post-World War II international price stabilization schemes. For coffee, price fluctuations were at least 50 percent greater during the agreement years from 1964 to 1972 than for the preceding nonagreement period from 1950 to 1963. The same result holds for sugar and cocoa. Apparently price stability increased only for wheat and tea during the tenure of international commodity agreements and these may have been due more to other factors (U.S. and Canadian production and stockpiling decisions) than to the agreements. However, it is difficult to determine whether the case is proved by these results. For example, it is possible that price fluctuations would have been even greater in the agreement period had the agreement not existed.

The evidence on the determinants of successful international cartel behavior have been reported by Behrman (1978, p. 64). A study of fifty-one attempts to organize international commodity markets yields the following results. The more successful were efforts in raising commodity prices, the fewer the number of producers; the higher the price elasticity of demand, the higher the income elasticity of demand for the commodity; the fewer the possibilities for short-term substitution of other commodities for the price in question, the larger the share of foreign control held by members of the agreement; the lower the differences in cost among producers in the agreement, the less the government involvement in the market. Most of these agree with our expectations, with the exception of high price elasticities of demand. Most industrial organization theory suggests that cartels will be more successful if demand is more inelastic. With high price elasticities of demand, there is an increasing incentive for a cartel member to cheat. For example, if the average cost of production is $5 per unit, the preagreement price was $8, and the agreement raises the price to $15, then each member would be tempted to maximize its own quantity of output at this high price. However, if each one increases output, the price will fall to a more competitive level.

The other results reported are more appealing. We expect successful agreements to have fewer producers since it is easier to detect a producer who cheats by increasing his output; we expect high income elasticities of demand for the product since this is a seller's market (the demand for these commodities grows more rapidly relative to overall income growth); we expect low short-run substitution since buyers have few alternatives and must simply pay the higher price for this commodity; we expect lower cost differences among producers since it is easier for members of a cartel to agree on the price they will wish to charge if they are similar in terms of costs; and we expect that lower government involvement helps a cartel since it will not have the buffer stocks to offset the actions of the cartel.

Success in raising price is only one aspect. A second measure of commodity cartel success is the longevity of the agreement. The same study of 51 international commodity agreements found that the average duration of the formal agreement was only 5.4 years and the median life was only 2.5 years. Using this second measure, it does not appear that most of the efforts were successful.

However, longevity of the agreement is an incomplete measure of the success of an agreement. For example, if the OPEC increase in the price of oil had lasted only two or three years, we would not have considered that attempt a failure since it would have transferred over $100 billion to the OPEC countries. The proper economic measure of cartel success is a combination of the two measures, namely, the amount of resources transferred from consuming countries to producing countries.

We conclude with three observations about commodity agreements. First, there is a natural tendency for economic forces to undo any agreement that raises price above the long-run competitive level. So long as supply can be increased by nonmembers of the cartel, buyers will switch their purchases from cartel members to this "competitive fringe" of suppliers. As purchases from cartel members drop, their incentive to stay with the cartel diminishes, and they will start cheating on the cartel price and increase their output. The same is true for agreements that reduce fluctuations in price. If fluctuations decrease, there is less uncertainty by suppliers and this stimulates increases in their output. If the international price stabilization scheme is controlled through a buffer stock, the increased supply necessitates increased purchases and additions to the buffer stock increase until the purchasing agents of the buffer stock run out of money. This leads to the breakup of the commodity agreement.

Second, we must be careful not to necessarily associate price stabilization with income stabilization. If the world price elasticity of demand for a commodity is unitary (meaning that a one percent increase in price would cause purchasers to drop the quantity purchased by one percent), then random supply fluctuations will be matched by equal and opposite price fluctuations so that income for suppliers as a whole will be stabilized by the market alone: If output drops by 10 percent of a crop failure in the supplying countries, price will rise by 10 percent in demanding countries. If an international commodity agreement which eliminated movements in price was reached, then export proceeds would vary directly with output and would have the same instability as output. In other words, price would not form the buffer against income fluctuations.

Commodity stabilization schemes are usually more successful in stabilizing income when most of the shocks to the international market are caused by shifts in the demand curve. They are less successful when output shifts are caused by supply shifts with unitary price elasticities of demand. Usually more variation in output occurs on the *supply* side for agricultural products because of weather conditions and other unforecastable events; output fluctuations in minerals and other nonagricultural products are caused by business cycles and *demand* considerations in purchasing countries. If this is true, we would expect that price stabilization schemes would be more successful in mineral and nonagricultural products (higher income elasticity items) than in agricultural products.

Third, we must be careful about drawing conclusions for international income distribution from the advent of successful commodity cartels. If a cartel succeeds in raising the price of a commodity exported from developing countries, there will be a redistribution of income from the rest of the world to these developing countries. While this would appear to make the international distribution of income more equal, it will not necessarily make the distribution of income more equal within the developing countries. For example, many studies of minimum wages find that there is a redistribution of income toward union labor and away from lower skilled (and poorer) nonunion labor. A similar result may hold for international commodity agreements. If output is restricted in a developing country and, as part of the world stabilization scheme, price raised, the output reduction and the price increase may benefit landowners and hurt wage earners in the exporting (developing) country. Thus, even though income had been redistributed from wealthy countries to poor countries by the price increase, the distribution of income within those developing countries may become more unequal. In each case, a careful study must be done in order to determine the overall redistributional effects.

REFERENCES

1. Behrman, Jere R., *Development, the International Economic Order, and Commodity Agreements.* Reading, Mass.: Addison-Wesley, 1978.

2. Hufbauer, Gary C., *Synthetic Materials and the Theory of International Trade.* Cambridge: Harvard University Press, 1966.

3. Kindleberger, Charles P., *Foreign Trade and the National Economy.* New Haven: Yale University Press, 1962, Ch. 3.

4. MacBean, Alistair, *Export Instability and Economic Development.* London: Allen & Unwin, 1966.

5. Magee, Stephen P. and Robins, Norman I., "The Raw Material Product Cycle," in Krause, Lawrence B. and Patrick, Hugh, eds., *Mineral Resources in the Pacific Area.* San Francisco: Federal Reserve Bank of San Francisco, 1978: 30–55.

6. Rosenberg, Nathan, "Innovative Responses to Materials Shortages," *American Economic Review* **63** (May 1973): 111–118.

7. Rowe, J.W.F., *Primary Commodities in International Trade.* Cambridge: Cambridge University Press, 1965.

International 5
Trade and the
Factors of
Production

We turn now to two important topics relating international trade to the factors of production. The first deals with the economic effects of trade on factor prices, the domestic distribution of income between capital and labor, trade and U.S. labor, the Cairnes' model, unions and international trade, and the Rybczynski theorem. The second relates the migration theory to the factors of production. In the first section, we assume that the factors of production are fixed but the goods move, while in the second section the markets are fixed but the factors move.

5.1 INTERNATIONAL TRADE AND THE FACTORS OF PRODUCTION

Factor Price Equalization

If all restrictions on immigration into the United States were eliminated, we know that U.S. wages would fall as workers from Mexico, Latin America, the Far East and other low-wage countries would enter rapidly. In 1948, Samuelson showed the remarkable result that even with complete prohibition of migration, real wages between the United States and the rest of the world would still be equalized (as if free migration were permitted) if there were free international trade in commodities. However, a fairly long list of sufficient (not necessary) conditions to guarantee this result include the following: the same production technology must be used worldwide; both regions must produce all goods; perfect competition must exist for both product and factor markets worldwide; and there must be no international transportation costs or trade barriers, such as quotas, tariffs, etc. In the presence of transportation costs and tariffs, there is merely a tendency for trade between high- and low-wage regions to push wages and other factor prices together; complete equalization does not occur.

We know that there is incomplete equalization of international wages because of national migration laws. Does, then, international trade provide enough pressure on high-wage countries to provide wage equalization? Table 5.1 shows hourly compensation in U.S. dollars for 31 countries. The results seem to refute the factor-price equalization theorem. It appears that U.S. workers earn almost 10 times as much as workers in Turkey; however, the numbers in this table overstate the international differences in wages. For example, the theorem asserts that wages will be equalized within each skill category, but U.S. workers differ considerably from Turkish workers because of the average skill difference. Thus the U.S. wage can be considered a combination of both a return on unskilled labor and a return on the amount of human capital which the U.S. worker has accumulated through his own and his ancestors' efforts. Another reason for the wage differences is that U.S. wage earners have more physical capital to work with than Turkish workers.

An indirect test of the factor-price equalization theorem might be performed by examining whether low-wage countries have more rapid wage increases than high-wage countries. Certainly if there were a tendency to equalize wages, this should be the case. An examination of the change in several countries' wage rates relative to those of the United States over a 10-year period are shown in Fig. 5.1. The results are consistent with the indirect test since they show that countries with low wages in 1967 tended to have more rapid wage increases.

The preceding results suggest another theory. The Heckscher-Ohlin model in Chapter 2 suggested that international trade permits countries to profit from their "long suit"; that is, capital-rich economies will have advantages over others in exporting capital-intensive goods. Similarly, labor-intensive economies can most efficiently export labor-intensive goods. In the absence of international trade, prices of goods that are labor intensive in production would be low in labor-abundant countries relative to capital-abundant countries. With the introduction of trade, international prices of identical goods will move together; that is, increase in labor-abundant countries and fall in capital-abundant countries. A similar phenomenon would occur for goods produced using capital-intensive production techniques: With the introduction of international trade, their prices would rise in capital-abundant economies and fall in capital-scarce economies. Trade will expand until the prices of capital-intensive goods are equalized worldwide or differ only by transportation costs. International trade flows will stabilize at levels consistent with equality of world supply

Table 5.1 Estimated hourly compensation in U.S. dollars of production workers in manufacturing for 31 countries, average of 1974, 1975, and 1976

Country		Country	
United States	$6.30	Denmark	$6.03
Canada	6.32	Finland	4.39
Argentina	1.77	France	4.19
Brazil	.80	Germany	6.09
Mexico	1.74	Greece	1.38
Australia	5.49	Ireland	2.47
Hong Kong	.72	Italy	4.04
Israel	1.94	Netherlands	6.18
Japan	3.00	Norway	5.21
Korea	.39	Portugal	1.37
Philippines	.28	Spain	2.15
Singapore	.71	Sweden	7.04
Sri Lanka	.24	Switzerland	5.85
Taiwan	.49	Turkey	.64
Austria	4.15	United Kingdom	3.10
Belgium	6.28		

Source: Unpublished data from the U.S. Department of Labor Statistics, Office of Productivity and Technology, (June 1977), "Estimated Hourly Compensation of Production Workers in Manufacturing, 31 Countries."

and demand. This framework suggests the following important implications for the relationship between international trade and factor markets.

The Stolper-Samuelson Theorem

Expansion of trade benefits the abundant factor in an economy and hurts the scarce factor. This theorem implies that unskilled labor in the United States would be hurt by trade expansion while skilled labor would benefit. This explains newspaper accounts of the AFL-CIO's opposition to freer trade. The Stolper-Samuelson theorem is intuitively appealing but it is deceptively powerful because it implies that unskilled labor in U.S. export industries will also oppose freer trade even though the industry will expand if trade is liberalized. The mechanics of the theorem operate as follows. The United States is skilled labor abundant and unskilled labor scarce relative to the rest of the world. Expansion of U.S. trade will permit more U.S. imports of textiles, bicycles, shoes, handicrafts, small cars, and other items,

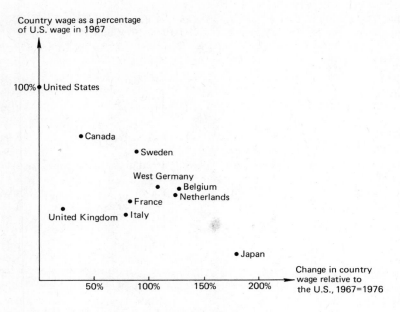

Country wage as a percentage of U.S. wage in 1967

100% • United States

• Canada

• Sweden

West Germany •   • Belgium
                 • Netherlands
        • France
United Kingdom • Italy

                              • Japan

Change in country wage relative to the U.S., 1967=1976

50%   100%   150%   200%

Fig. 5.1   Wage levels and wage changes, 1967–1976

but it will depress the U.S. price of these goods, forcing producers of shoes in New England and textiles in the South to close down. Factory closings would result in the release of many unskilled laborers but only a few skilled laborers. In the long run, these workers will be reabsorbed by the labor market or they will drop out of the labor force. Since trade expansion also means that U.S. exports will increase because foreigners will buy more U.S. exports with decreased tariffs abroad, export industries will absorb some of the labor released by the cutback in import-competing industries. But U.S. export industries are skilled-labor intensive (see the discussion in Chapter 3). Increased production of export goods requires a lot of skilled labor, and only a little unskilled labor. Thus the export industry needs a lot of skilled labor to expand but only a few are available. In contrast, it needs only a few more unskilled laborers, but many of them are available. The small flow of skilled labor out of textiles and the large demand for skilled labor to expand, for example, aerospace exports, generates upward pressure on the wages of skilled labor. Conversely, the large flow of unskilled labor out of textiles coupled with the small increase in demand for them in aerospace industries causes downward pressure on unskilled labor wages.

These wage changes have several effects. The changes are required to lure additional skilled workers from the import-competing industry into export industries, and they serve to choke off the excessive movement of unskilled workers which simply cannot be employed (some of the latter drop out of the labor force—especially nonprimary family wage earners). But for all workers who stay in the labor force, the wage changes induce the export industries to alter their production techniques away from skilled labor and toward unskilled labor. As the skilled-labor wages rise and unskilled-labor wages fall, profits can clearly be made by shifting production techniques toward the cheaper form.

A good historical example of how trade expansion benefits the abundant factor is provided by Japan. For many years, Japan has been a labor-abundant economy. From the 1920s until past mid-century, its principal exports included silk, cotton textiles, toys, and other labor-intensive goods. Since the 1950s, it has moved into automobiles, electronics, steel, cameras, and goods requiring both capital and labor. From 1960 to 1975, the Japanese wage (expressed in dollars) rose from 10 percent to 48 percent of the U.S. wage. In recent years, Japanese firms have been increasingly active on the Asian continent—Korea, Taiwan, and Hong Kong—to economize on the "high cost of Japanese labor." The extraordinary rise in Japanese GNP coupled with the even more rapid growth of Japanese exports has been accompanied by an increase in the relative improvement of labor in Japan.

Trade and U.S. Labor

Statistical evidence indicates that U.S. tariffs keep out goods that are unskilled-labor intensive. Fig. 5.2 and Table 5.2 from a study by Ball on the effects of protection show that effective U.S. tariffs are higher for low-wage U.S. industries than for high-wage industries. If all U.S. tariffs were dropped, prices would probably fall more in the United States for low-wage goods than for high-wage goods. As a result, unskilled labor would be hurt more than skilled labor.

The statistics just noted refer only to import-competing industries. Consider all U.S. industries. In 1967, manufacturing wage rates in import-competing industries were $2.60 per hour compared with $2.84 per hour in all U.S. manufacturing and $3.16 in U.S. export industries (Magee, 1972: 649). Thus trade restrictions permit expansion of import-competing industries and protect low-wage labor. Trade expansion would encourage exports and benefit high-wage labor.

Consider, finally, the short-term effects of cutting tariffs on workers displaced by imports. A study of displaced workers, who were laid off in

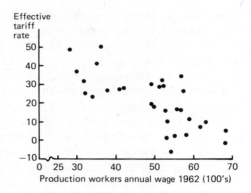

Fig. 5.2. 1962 effective tariff rates and annual wage of production workers in thirty-one U.S. industries.

Table 5.2 Comparison of U.S. industries with 1962 effective tariffs greater and less than 20 percent*

	Average annual wage all employees (1)	Average annual wage, production workers (2)	Wages' share of value added percent) (3)
1. All U.S. operating manufacturing establishments	$5,557	$4,875	50.11
2. 31 industries	5,565	4,876	51.90
	(5,510)	(4,917)	(52.08)
3. 15 industries with effective tariffs less than 20 percent	6,334	5,703	52.98
	(6,334)	(5,709)	(52.16)
4. 16 industries with effective tariffs greater than 20 percent	4,637	4,002	50.22
	(4,738)	(4,174)	(52.02)

*The uninclosed values are weighted averages, for example, in row 2, Col. (1), $5,565 is all wages divided by all employment in the 31 industries. The values in parentheses are averages of the industry values, for example, $5,510 is the sum of the industry values divided by 31. Ball (April, 1967, p. 185)

1969 and 1970 and interviewed in February 1972, showed that they had the following characteristics [Bale (1976)]:

- The average age was 44 years.
- Eleven percent were over 60 years old.
- Fifty-one percent were male.
- Ninety-one percent were whites.
- The average education was 8.5 grades (27 percent had gone through grade 12, and 5 percent had gone to college).
- Fifty-six percent were employed, 27 percent were actively seeking work and 14 percent had retired or were not planning to reenter the labor force within the next year.
- Before displacement, they earned $3.02 per hour; those employed at the time of the survey earned $2.68 per hour (both in 1972 prices, implying a cut of 11 percent).
- Sixty-nine percent were the primary wage earner in the family.
- The average duration of unemployment was 251 days.
- Lump-sum payments to these laborers provided by the 1962 Trade Expansion Act equalled $746.

Thus the major costs to labor displaced by U.S. imports were: 251 days of unemployment, at least an 11 percent drop in the hourly wage upon reemployment, and roughly a 14 percent chance of dropping out of the labor force altogether. We turn next to an alternative to the Stolper-Samuelson model.

The Cairnes Model

Cairnes developed the theory of noncompeting groups. The theory states that labor does not really compete among industries. Thus what happens to wages in one industry depends only on the price of output in that industry and is unrelated to wage changes in the rest of the economy. The implication of this theory for the relationship between trade and the factors of production is that labor in export industries should favor restrictive trade. This contrasts with the Stolper-Samuelson model, which implies that each factor of production will adopt a position that is independent of whether the industry is import-competing or export: The abundant factor favors free trade and the other factor opposes it.

A statistical examination of the data also provides support for the Cairnes view. Table 5.3 shows how the average trade balance in a number of U.S. industries is related to the lobbying position of either capital (through lobbying trade associations) or labor (through the action of unions). Notice that those industries in which capital favors protectionism are basically import-competing, with $254 million in trade deficits, whereas industries in which capital prefers free trade are export industries, with positive net exports of $689 million. The same pattern is true of labor. Industries in which unions prefer protectionism have $321 million in trade deficits (import-competing) while those preferring free trade tend to be export industries, with $985 million in trade surpluses. In both cases, the differences in the trade balances are significant. All things considered, the evidence supports the Cairnes model more strongly than the Stolper-Samuelson approach in explaining how international trade affects factor markets [see Magee (11)].

Table 5.3   Average industry trade balance in 1967 (millions of $) related to lobbying positions of capital and labor in 1973 on the trade bill

	Industry trade balance	Number of industries
Position of capital (trade associations)		
Prefer protectionism	$-254	15
Prefer free-trade	689	9
Position of labor (unions)		
Prefer protectionism	-321	16
Prefer free-trade	985	5

Unions and International Trade

When transportation costs are small and international trade is unrestricted, it is difficult for sellers with market power to charge monopoly prices for goods. For example, if one firm corners the market in automobiles in the United States and attempts to charge prohibitively high prices, foreign suppliers will undercut the price, thereby making it very difficult for the practice to continue.

A similar phenomenon exists with factor markets: If labor unions attempt to keep their wages artificially high, then foreign goods produced by cheaper labor will be imported and displace local production. For example, the United Auto Workers push up wages, causing auto imports to increase and displace local production. Thus in factor markets as well as in product markets, foreign trade provides a check on the ability of any group to exercise long-term market power. In fact, some unusual results can be derived when this occurs.

The Factor Market Power Paradox

Free trade builds in incentives for factors not to press for higher wages in certain industries. Assume that the United Auto Workers introduces a 10 percent higher wage in the auto industry than in all other industries. Assume also that it attempts to maintain a 10 percent differential no matter what happens to wages in the rest of the economy. If automobiles are more labor-intensive in production than the average good in the economy, this will deal a severe blow to the automobile industry. The reason is that it has faced an increase in the cost of one of its most important factors of production. As automobile production is cut back and workers are laid off, there is a large amount of labor unemployed relative to capital and other factors. These cannot be reabsorbed into the rest of the economy without a decrease in wages in the rest of the economy. If the price of automobiles is held at a competitive level by imports, then all of the adjustment to the wage increase in the automobile industry must be absorbed by changes in employment and output. In the new long-run equilibrium, *wages will fall by more than 10 percent compared with the rest of the economy, so that even inclusive of the union differential real wages will have fallen in the auto industry.* The reason for this paradoxical result is that if a factor attempts to increase its return in an industry in which it is the intensive factor, it puts the industry, which is the most important employer of that factor, out of business. The implication is that labor unions would be better off if they organized and put capital-intensive, rather than labor-intensive industries out of business (see Magee, 1976, p. 28). The general rule of thumb is that a factor attempting to make itself better off should try to raise its return in industries in which it is the nonintensive factor of production. By putting these industries out of business, it encourages the expansion of labor-intensive industries and bids up both its own wages and, possibly, wages elsewhere in the economy.

There are many examples of how markets' power by factors of production have reduced output in domestic industries. For example, in the 1960s, the guilds in Hollywood raised returns to both actors and skilled labor to prohibitively high levels. The result was a closing down of some of the largest Hollywood studios and a major movement abroad by American filmmakers. Films were shot in Spain and Italy, then imported into the United States. International trade thus provided a safety valve for what was becoming a prohibitively expensive operation.

Another example concerns the U.S. corporate sector relative to the noncorporate sector (see Magee, 1976, pp. 97–98). The data indicate that the corporate sector is more labor intensive than the noncorporate sector in the United States. Labor's share of output is 83 percent in the corporate sector, and only 58 percent in the noncorporate sector. Paradoxically, it is easier for labor unions to organize in the corporate sector because of large-scale plants which make union organization less costly than in the small-business sector. However, raising wages in the corporate sector relative to the noncorporate sector may provide substantial offsets in that the businesses cut back because of demands for higher wages are those industries that employ a large amount of labor. Thus, unions can create both downward pressure on wages in the economy as a whole, as well as cause some sectoral unemployment problems by pushing up wages in the labor-intensive areas.

Unions and Comparative Advantage

The effects of unions on international trade patterns are fairly straight-forward. Any factor attempting to raise its return in the export sector relative to the rest of the economy will lower output in that sector. This will reduce exports as well as imports. If output is lowered sufficiently in the export sector, the country may actually start to import the goods, so that the pattern of trade is reversed. Thus the traditional comparative advantage theories explaining international trade patterns (Ricardo, Heckscher-Ohlin, etc., discussed in Chapter 2) will have very little predictive power in economies in which the export industry pays more for either factor of production than does the import-competing industry.

We turn now to an examination of the economic effects of factor movements. Whenever prices are fixed, economic adjustments occur through changes in output—advertising and waiting in line, to name a few. Consider a small open economy which has no restrictions on international trade and which is not large enough to influence the world's price in any given market. This means that the country has a small share among world buyers for its imports and a small share among world sellers for its exports. But, saying that an economy is small does not guarantee that it will not influence world prices in some markets: Switzerland accounts for a small percent of developed country gross national product but a larger percent of developed country watches.

If there were an influx of, say, labor into a small open economy, wages would temporarily be depressed. Both manufacturing and agriculture would presumably benefit from this situation. But would both industries expand? Not necessarily since there is the same fixed amount of physical capital to be allocated between them. It is clear that the labor-intensive sector (manufacturing) would expand. But does the capital-intensive sector (agriculture) expand or contract? The following solution to this problem was provided in 1954.

The Rybczynski Theorem

Rybczynski (1954) found that an inflow of one factor of production into a small open economy will cause the sector using that factor intensively to expand and the other sector to contract. Thus, in the previous problem, *an influx of labor will expand manufacturing but contract agriculture.* The reasoning is that if labor becomes cheaper, profits in manufacturing will rise relative to those in agriculture since labor is more important in the former. Expansion of manufacturing will then absorb much of the labor inflow but not all of it.

Manufacturing must also get capital equipment from somewhere. Since all of the capital in the economy is already fully employed, it must lure capital away from agriculture if it is to expand. Thus, compared to the prelabor-inflow situation, agriculture now finds itself with more labor but less capital. Since labor is less important than capital in its production, its output must fall.

Rybczynski also showed that if wages change relative to capital costs, the price of manufacturing must change relative to agricultural products. But relative prices cannot change on world markets because of our assumption that this economy is small. Thus, in the new equilibrium, wages must be bid back to their prelabor inflow levels. In short, when labor flows into an economy, we know that labor-intensive industries will expand, capital-intensive industries will contract, and in the long run there will be no change in wages relative to capital prices.

5.2 MIGRATION THEORY

An example of factor migration is the multinational corporation, which moves capital into countries to produce goods to sell locally. Automobile plants in Australia, Latin America, and Western Europe, which were built by U.S. firms fit this case (see Chapter 3 for different theories explaining multinational corporation behavior). Another example is international racing teams, which move labor (racing drivers) and variable capital (their cars) to combine with fixed local capital (racetracks) to serve largely local markets (fans). The Grand Prix racing circuit includes countries in Europe and South America, South Africa, Japan, and the United States. Scientists and engineers (human capital) also move internationally, mainly from developing to developed countries to earn higher incomes. Let us consider this last case.

The Brain Drain

It is said that there are more Pakistani doctors in London than there are in all of Pakistan. Between 1962 and 1971, over 200,000 professionals and technicians immigrated into the United States from the developing countries. The developing countries also lost 40,000 professionals to Canada between 1963 and 1972 and 60,000 to the United Kingdom between 1964 and 1972 (see Hamada, 1977, p. 125). Hamada argues that the U.S. Immigration Act of 1975, which eliminated the earlier racial-origin quotas, has reinforced the brain drain from developing countries.

There is a policy debate over whether the brain drain should be permitted or whether the developing-country nationals should be encouraged to stay at home (Johnson, 1975, Chapter 6). Those who favor letting skilled labor migrate throughout the world, that is, those favoring continuation of the brain drain, make the following arguments. First, the migrants may simply be seeking to escape from political instability and victimization by their home governments. Forcing them to stay at home would not discourage arbitrary harsh treatment of all persons by heavy-handed home governments. Second, like any profit-motivated activity, the brain drain should increase world output since factors move from low-wage areas to high-wage areas. For example, if a Pakistani doctor moves to the United States and his annual earnings increase from $15,000 to $35,000, world output is increased by $20,000. Third, proponents of limiting the brain drain take too parochial a view of the world: To count as Pakistan's wealth only the economic activity going on within its geographical borders is wrong. If a Pakistani doctor can earn a much higher salary outside his country of birth, then the Pakistani welfare really increases by letting him go. The correct way to measure developing-country GNP according to this argument is by summing up the income of all of its residents anywhere in the world rather than just those residing in their country of birth. Fourth, by working in a more competitive environment, scientists and doctors from developing countries are able to keep their knowledge more current than if they are forced to stay at home.

There are, however, good arguments for restricting the brain drain. First, the highly educated in the developing countries were educated largely by taxpayers in those countries. If these doctors practice medicine in the United States, their incomes are taxed in the United States, and the developing-country citizens, who subsidized the training of doctors, are never paid back. While the arrangement would be complicated, this problem could be solved by either tax treaties or loan arrangements for education. Second, the difference between the highly skilled person's income in the developing countries and in the developed countries overstates how much world income would increase if he is permitted to migrate. If he creates more externalities, such as nonreimbursed benefits, in the developing country than in the developed country, these may offset the private income differential. For example, in the case cited earlier, if the

Pakistani doctor indirectly generated $20,000 per year in benefits for which he is not compensated by staying home in Pakistan, then world output would not increase if he left Pakistan. These indirect benefits might include keeping the Pakistani labor force more healthy, inspiring young Pakistanis to get better educations, overcoming the diseconomies of scale of having too small a scientific or medical community in Pakistan, etc.

The issue is clearly a complicated one. The story of Dr. Livingston in Africa summarizes well some of the dilemmas faced by educated developing-country nationals. By being in Africa, Livingston helped low-income people at the expense of his private income since he would have made more money in Europe. His medical training depreciated, like any other capital asset, because he did not stay in touch with medical advances in Europe. But the benefits he generated for others in Africa undoubtedly exceeded his private income loss. This example would argue for restricting the brain drain. But equally important, is the observation that Livingston voluntarily made his decision to go to Africa.

REFERENCES

1. Bale, Malcolm D., "Estimates of Trade-Displacement Costs for U.S. Workers," *Journal of International Economics* **6** (August 1976): 245–250.

2. Ball, David S., "United States Effective Tariffs and Labor's Share," *Journal of Political Economy* **75** (April 1967): 183–187.

3. Cairnes, J.E., *Some Leading Principles of Political Economy*. London: Macmillan, 1874.

4. Hamada, Koichi, "Taxing the Brain Drain: A Global Point of View," in Bhagwati, J., ed., *The New International Economic Order: The North-South Debate*. Cambridge, Mass.: MIT Press, 1977: 125–155.

5. Johnson, Harry G., *Technology and Economic Interdependence*. London: St. Martin's, 1975, Ch. 6.

6. Magee, Stephen P., "The Welfare Effects of Restrictions on U.S. Trade," *Brookings Papers on Economic Activity* (No. 3, 1972): 645–701.

7. ——— "Factor Market Distortions, Production and Trade: A Survey," *Oxford Economic Papers* **25** (March 1973): 1–43.

8. ———, *International Trade and Distortion in Factor Markets*. New York: Marcel Dekker, 1976.

9. ———, "Jobs and the Multinational Corporation: The Home-Country Perspective," in Hawkins, Robert G., ed., *Research in International Business and Finance*, Greenwich, Conn.: JAI Press, 1979, Ch. 1: 1–23.

10. ———, "Twenty Paradoxes in International Trade Theory," in Hillman, Jimmye S. and Schmitz, Andrew J., eds., *International Trade and Agriculture:*

Agriculture: Problems and Policies. Lincoln: University of Nebraska Press, *Problems and Policies.* Lincoln: University of Nebraska Press, 1979: 91–115.

11. ———, "Three Simple Tests of the Stolper-Samuelson Theorem," in Oppenheimer, Peter, ed., *Current Issues in World Trade and Payments.* London: Routledge and Kegan Paul, 1979.

12. Rybczynski, T.M., "Factor Endowment and Relative Commodity Prices," *Economica, N.S.* **22** (November 1955): 336–341.

13. Samuelson, Paul A., "International Trade and the Equalization of Factor Prices," *Economic Journal* **58** (June 1948): 163–184.

14. Stolper, Wolfgang F. and Samuelson, Paul A., "Protection and Real Wages," *Review of Economic Studies* **9** (November 1941): 58–73.

Politics and   6
International
Trade Policy

In this chapter we discuss five important areas where politics and national policy interact with international trade. The first area is the determination of tariffs and commercial policy, which will be discussed in 6.1. In this section we examine several issues concerning tariff policies: the alliance between political parties and either free trade or protection, which factors of production will favor protection and which will not, the analysis of the economic welfare costs of tariffs and the redistribution effects, and national policy on the dumping of foreign goods in the local economy. The second area, which will be discussed in section 6.2, is the economic and political determination of the economic integration of nation states.

Section 6.3 analyzes balance of trade policy. The mercantilists used to think that by running an export surplus they could get rich. While this might be true for an individual, for the nation as a whole, accumulation of gold for its own sake is not a wise policy if the gold is never consumed in terms of economic goods. This section also covers some economic determinants of trade balances: differential income elasticities and the monetary model. Empirical evidence on desequilibria is reflected in deviations from purchasing power parity. A historical example of the trade-imbalance problem is provided by the Opium Wars. These wars were caused by persistent trade balance deficits in the three-way trade between India, Britain, and China. Section 6.4 considers economic and political theories of economic imperialism. Section 6.5 explores the relationship between international trade and economic development.

6.1 TARIFF POLICY

In the late 19th and early 20th centuries Republicans were known as
protectionists because they promoted the McKinley Tariff and other
tariffs. This phenomenon is explained by the fact that the United States was
industrializing and its young industries were not yet strong enough to
compete with their older rivals in Britain and Western Europe. Using the
infant-industry argument for tariffs, U.S. entrepreneurs sought to keep the
price of European manufactured goods sold in the United States high so
that their goods would not be undercut. For this reason the tariff rates on
dutiable imports *averaged* over 50 percent (see Fig. 6.1); that is, if it cost
$100 to produce an item in Europe, when it entered the United States a $50
tax had to be paid by the U.S. importer. In equilibrium, the difference
between the European price and the U.S. price of the good might differ by
as much as 50 percent. This contrasts with the pattern of political alliance in
the United States in the postwar period. Today, U.S. industry has matured
so that its existence no longer depends on tariffs to protect it from imported
goods.

However, organized labor is worried about protecting the high wages
it obtains from union action because high-wage goods can be displaced by
low-wage imports from developing countries. The pressure for protection
has switched from the Republicans to the Democrats since the latter draws
much of its support from organized labor. In the early 1970s, the Burke-
Hartke bill, which would have cut U.S. imports by over one-third to
protect blue-collar wages from low-wage import goods, was proposed by a
large segment of labor and supported by a number of Democrats. Part of
the economic motivation for the bill was the "overvaluation of the dollar"
in the late 1960s, meaning that U.S. prices were higher than exchange-rate
adjusted prices of foreign goods. Thus one of the most important
motivations for tariffs can be found in the attempts by the factors of
production to improve their income. As we noted in Chapter 5, the Stolper-
Samuelson Theorem suggests that increases in tariff levels will increase the
real income of the factor of production used intensively in import-
competing production and lower the real income of the factor of
production used intensively in export industries. Since the United States
appears to have a relative abundance of skilled labor and a relative
shortage of unskilled labor, it would appear that trade restrictions would
help unskilled labor since it would limit imports of low-wage goods and
hurt skilled labor since foreign countries would retaliate with tariffs on
U.S. exports. Given this situation, a lot of highly paid scientists and
engineers employed in export industries would eventually be hurt.

Another motivation for protection is the *optimum tariff*. When
countries levy tariffs, prices rise to their consumers but the amount paid to

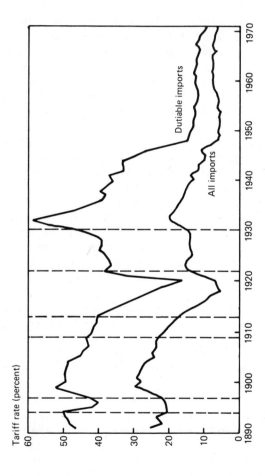

Source: U.S. Tariff Commission, tabulation, "Value of U.S. Imports for Consumption, Duties Collected, and Ratio of Duties to Values, under the Tariff Act of 1930, 1930–71" (March 1972; processed). The tariffs that apply are embodied in the following laws:

1890–94: McKinley law	1897–1909: Dingley law	1922–30: Fordney-McCumber law
1894–97: Wilson law	1909–13: Payne-Aldrich law	1930–71: Smoot-Hawley law
	1913–22: Underwood law	

Source: Magee (1972, p. 656)

Fig. 6.1   U.S. tariff rates, 1890–1971

foreign suppliers falls. Thus foreigners pay part of the tax. Table 6.1 shows
how a country's welfare can be made to increase by levying such a tariff.
The share of imports in U.S. GNP is about 5 percent; if the elasticity of
foreign demand for U.S. goods is about 2 percent, then U.S. economic
welfare increases by only .7 percent if the United States imposes a 100
percent tariff *and* if foreigners do not retaliate and levy higher tariffs on
U.S. exports.

A third motivation for tariffs is to stimulate aggregate employment.
Tariffs can add to a country's total employment in the short run by
stimulating job creation in import-competing industries. If the economy is
already at full employment, however, the relative increase in the price of
imported goods simply alters the composition of employment among
industries. There are a number of arguments against the use of tariffs for
this type of policy. First, they are not as efficient as macroeconomic tools of
monetary and fiscal policy. Second, they are a "begger thy neighbor" policy
since they force unemployment on foreigners. Nevertheless, in the troughs
of business cycles, the employment argument becomes a strong one for
protectionist forces. This was true in the Burke-Hartke discussions in the
U.S. Congress in the early 1970s. It was also true when Congress passed the
Tariff Act of 1930, which increased duties on more than 1000 articles
imported into the United States. Many countries attempted to export their
unemployment in a similar manner: Within a year of the passage of this act,
25 foreign countries had raised their tariffs on U.S. goods. This retaliatory
action is called a *tariff war*. In addition to the great depression, the tariff
war also contributed to the decline in world trade from $65 billion in 1929
to less than $25 billion in 1933.

A fourth argument for tariffs is that they can improve a country's trade
balance and balance of payments. An increase in import prices caused by
the tariff reduces the value of imports and improves the trade balance in the
short run. Several factors modify this effect, however. First, retaliation
against the country's exports may result. Second, there are indirect
reductions in the value of exports through other mechanisms: The rise in
the price of imports discourages production of goods that use these imports
as inputs and encourages the movement of factors out of the export
industries and into import-competing industries. This causes a rise in the
price of exports and of nontraded goods. Finally, the reduction in the value
of imports into the country reduces the foreign exchange earnings of the
rest of the world and hence reduces its ability to purchase the country's
exports.

The use of the tariff as a means of improving the trade balance and the
balance of payments is also symptomatic of the failure of other more
general mechanisms to achieve international adjustment of payments

Table 6.1 Relative welfare gain from optimum tariff policies
Percent

Elasticity of foreign demand	Optimum tariff $t = \dfrac{100}{\eta - 1}$ (percent)	Import share under free trade									
		0.05	0.10	0.15	0.20	0.25	0.30	0.35	0.40	0.45	0.50
1.10	1000	3.4	6.7	9.9	12.8	15.3	18.1	20.3	22.8	23.7	24.8
1.20	500	2.6	5.1	7.4	9.6	11.7	13.5	15.0	16.3	17.3	18.0
1.30	333	2.1	4.1	6.0	7.6	9.2	10.6	11.7	12.6	13.4	13.8
1.40	250	1.8	3.4	4.9	6.3	7.5	8.6	9.5	10.2	10.7	11.1
1.50	200	1.5	2.8	3.8	5.2	6.2	7.1	7.8	8.4	8.9	9.1
1.75	133	0.9	1.8	2.5	3.4	4.1	4.7	5.2	5.6	5.8	6.1
2.00	100	0.7	1.4	2.0	2.6	3.1	3.4	3.8	4.1	4.3	4.4
2.25	80	0.6	1.1	1.5	2.0	2.3	2.6	2.9	3.1	3.2	3.3
2.50	66	0.5	0.9	1.2	1.6	1.8	2.1	2.3	2.4	2.5	2.6
2.75	57	0.4	0.7	1.0	1.3	1.5	1.7	1.8	1.9	2.0	2.1
3.00	50	0.3	0.6	0.8	1.0	1.2	1.4	1.5	1.6	1.7	1.7
3.50	40	0.2	0.4	0.6	0.7	0.9	1.0	1.1	1.1	1.2	1.2
4.00	33	0.2	0.3	0.4	0.6	0.7	0.7	0.8	0.9	0.9	0.9
4.50	28	0.1	0.2	0.3	0.4	0.5	0.6	0.6	0.7	0.7	0.7
5.00	20	0.1	0.2	0.3	0.4	0.4	0.5	0.5	0.5	0.6	0.5

Source: Reproduced from Harry G. Johnson, "The Gain from Exploiting Monopoly or Monopsony Power in International Trade," *Economica,* Vol. 35, New Series (May 1968), p. 156, reprinted in Harry G. Johnson, *Aspects of the Theory of Tariffs* (London: George Allen and Unwin, 1971).

imbalances. There is good reason to be skeptical about the use of tariffs for providing a long-run solution to any country's balance-of-payments problem. Since balance-of-payments disequilibria may be attributable to a monetary disequilibrium, tariffs are clearly not an effective mechanism for dealing with this situation. When a balance-of-payments deficit is caused by the expansion of domestic money exceeding the expansion in the domestic demand for money, the balance-of-payments deficit may simply be the market adjusting to monetary disequilibria. Since tariffs change the relative prices of goods and affect the demand for money only in the short run, they cannot provide a solution to a long-term monetary disturbance.

The Economic Costs of Tariffs

The most important principle of tariff analysis is that the economic welfare cost of a tariff increases with the square of the tariff. (We assume foreigners retaliate if the country tries to levy an optimum tariff.) For example, if the tariff increases from 10 to 20 percent, then the economic welfare cost increases fourfold. If the tariff increases from 20 to 40 percent, then the economic welfare cost increases another fourfold, so that a 40 percent tariff has 16 times as much economic distoriton as a 10 percent tariff.

The economic welfare costs created by tariffs come from two sources. The first is the distortion of consumer preferences. Since a tariff artificially raises prices, people who would have purchased the good do not and therefore lose in welfare because of the presence of the artificially high price. However, the home country does not lose the entire increased cost of the imported good since it collects tariff revenue which goes to the government. The second distortion is on production in the United States: A tariff on U.S. imports of textiles causes distortion of U.S. production toward goods produced more efficiently abroad.

The implication is that at low-tariff levels, the welfare costs of tariffs are low. For example, for over $10 billion of U.S. trade in imports in 1971, which competes directly with U.S. production, the welfare costs of the 8 percent tariff were between $300 and $800 million. These imports accounted for one-fourth of 1971 U.S. imports. However, the redistribution effects of even such small tariffs are high. An 8 percent tariff on goods competing directly with U.S. production had a small welfare cost but it redistributed $1.35 to $1.87 billion from consumers of imported goods to producers of these goods. Since this is a redistribution of income within the United States, it is not considered a cost to the country as a whole.

An interesting aspect of tariffs is that in the long run, factor movements can eventually eliminate the welfare costs. For example, a tariff on shoe imports into the United States leads to larger investments in U.S. shoe production by foreign firms. If enough capital is employed in the shoe industry in the United States, the price of shoes relative to other goods will eventually move back toward the pretariff level.

6.2 ECONOMIC INTEGRATION

The organizational forms of economic integration range from free trade areas, to customs unions, to a common market, and finally, to complete economic integration. In a free trade area, the members have no tariffs among one another, but each has its own set of tariffs and quantitative restrictions vis-à-vis the rest of the world. The customs union is a free trade area but with member countries establishing identical tariff rates on each product imported from outside. A common market is a customs union with no restrictions on the movement of the factors of production. The highest stage, the economic union, is a single economy with a unified fiscal and monetary policy, and a single currency.

The economic basis of a customs union is a common external tariff. Tariffs are taxes on trade which affect the optimal allocation of resources among countries, the pattern of consumption, terms of trade, and income distribution. As a direct effect, tariffs reduce both the volume of imports and the price paid to the exporter, and they usually improve the balance of payments and terms of trade, at least in the short run. The higher the importer's elasticity of demand and the lower the exporter's elasticity of supply, the greater the improvement of the terms of trade. Thus the tariff-levying country captures part of the world income which would have gone to foreign producers.

This international redistribution of income hurts foreigners and produces retaliations which result in all countries establishing similar levels of tariffs. In 1975, for example, the trade weighted average on industrial goods tariffs were as follows: Japan 7.1%, U.S.A. 7.5%, EEC 10.1%.

The economic welfare effects of customs unions are discussed under two headings: trade creation and trade diversion. Recall that a customs union drops the tariffs on imports from member states but maintains unified tariffs vis-à-vis others. *Trade diversion* occurs if one of the members becomes the cheapest producer after the union was formed, taking away business from the low-cost world producer outside the union. Thus diversion stands for the welfare cost of a shift from a low-cost to a higher-cost producer, which means a global welfare loss. Take the following case as an illustration. The cost of producing a ton of steel is $100 in Germany, $150 in Belgium, and $250 in the Netherlands. Both German and Belgian steel face a 100 percent import duty in the Netherlands, which makes the ton of German steel worth $200 and the Belgian steel worth $300. The Germans are the relative low-cost producer at $200/ton and get the lion's share of the Dutch market. Now, if the Netherlands and Belgium were to form a customs union, Belgian steel would be exempted from Dutch tariffs and become the relative low-cost producer at $150/ton. The Dutch would switch to Belgian steel and the consequence would be a diversion of output from the low-cost German to the high-cost Belgian steel. The welfare cost occurs because the economic decision of steel importers is distorted by artificial political barriers to trade.

Trade creation works the opposite way: Trade is created if the union contains the previously discriminated against low-cost producer, which would become the supplier of the union. If the Netherlands had formed a customs union with Germany instead, no trade would have switched sources and the Netherlands would import even more steel than before. The drop in the tariff is like a reduction in transportation costs and permits trade to expand. The welfare gain of the expansion in trade is called *trade creation.*

There are two different models of how countries can integrate: the economic models of Balassa and others and the neighbors of neighbors theory from political science.

The Economic Theory of Customs Unions

The economic theory of customs unions asserts that there are four primary gains to participating countries: production and consumption efficiency gains, gains from breaking up oligopolistic industry structures, gains from expanding economies of scale, and gains from free movements of capital and labor. An economic approach would suggest that the more important these four considerations are to countries, the more likely they are to form a customs union.

First, the production and consumption efficiency gains from a customs union emanate from reduced tariffs on trade among members of the union. The reduced tariffs provide goods at lower costs to consumers in the importing region and they stimulate movements of resources out of import-competing production and into more efficient production for export, (that is, into product areas in which the country has a greater comparative advantage). The welfare gains to consumers from more efficient consumption and the reallocation of production provide examples of trade creation. There is an offsetting consideration, however. If Germany and France enter into a customs union (the European Economic Community) and Germany switches its purchases from the United States to France because there is now no tariff on French shipments into Germany, then Germany is worse off to the extent that it pays France a higher price for the same goods that it used to buy from the United States. For example, if Germany used to pay the United States $5 for a good and there was a 60 percent tariff on the good in Germany so that the cost to German consumers was $8, and the French cost of the good is $8 after the customs union is formed, then there is trade diversion loss equal to $3 for Germany. Because Germany entered into the customs union the $3 that used to be paid by German consumers to the German government through the tariff on imports from the United States, which ultimately benefited German citizens, is now being paid to French producers. The issue for customs union theory is whether this trade diversion is more or less than the efficiency gains from trade creation. Some empirical estimates of the trade creation efficiency gains resulting from formation of the European Economic Community are almost exactly equal to the welfare losses from trade diversion. Thus, from a pure efficiency standpoint it does not appear that the formation of the European Economic Community was significant. The problem with the calculation of net gains from trade creation and trade diversion is that they are rather poor predictors of how countries might coalesce into customs unions.

A second potential gain from a customs union is that oligopolistic industry structures which have grown up in an economy can be broken down by the stimulus of outside competition. For example, when Germany and France entered into the Common Market, import-competing producers in both countries felt increased competition from producers in the other country. Large firms in concentrated industries sometimes set high prices for their products and shared part of the gain with strong labor unions. This inefficient behavior is reduced by expansion of the market and increased competition. Unfortunately, this consideration also is not particularly helpful in predicting which countries will successfully join one another in a customs union. Since political power tends to be greater for oligopolistic industries and their labor unions, they will oppose formation of a customs union because it would erode their economic power.

The third gain from customs union formation is exploitation of economies of scale. A number of studies have shown that many European countries are too small to support the size of plant needed to yield minimum average costs of production. As the size of a market increases, firms are able to increase plant size so as to exploit these economies of large-scale production. This consideration suggests that smaller countries will gain more from customs union formation than large countries. Casual empiricism suggests that this is certainly the case.

Fourth, there is increased efficiency with customs union formation because it permits freer movements of capital and labor. For example, Europe experienced the migration of low-wage Italian workers into Germany to take advantage of a higher demand for labor. This benefited German producers, who had an increased supply of labor, as well as the Italian workers, who were able to obtain higher wages. Similarly, with an expanded factor market, producers were able to move capital in the European Economic Community to more efficient locations. We would expect that the larger the differences in wages among economies and the more inefficiently allocated plant locations are because of restrictions on ownership and movement, the greater the gains to be had from a customs union and hence the more likely two countries would be to coalesce. This factor would predict that high-wage countries and low-wage countries would be more likely to form a customs union. A casual review of the European Community does not provide strong evidence on this point.

The Neighbors of Neighbors Theory

This theory from international relations suggests that neighbors are "natural" enemies, while the neighbors of neighbors are friends. Kautilya, a third century Indian politician, developed the theory of natural enemies in his book *Arthashastra*. His theory became a blueprint for the unification of ancient India. The pattern was for noncontiguous states to unify by putting pressure on states in-between. Jay and Hamilton subscribed to this theory of natural enemies in the *Federalist Papers*, Nos. 5–8. The theory can be loosely applied to the coalition of nation states that participated in World War II. Germany attacked all of its contiguous neighbors, with the exception of Switzerland: Poland, Czechoslovakia, Austria, France, Belgium, the Netherlands, and Denmark. Before the war started, Germany was an ally of or friendly with countries that did not touch it but that were neighbors with these countries: the Soviet Union, Spain, and Italy. Other noncontiguous sympathizers with the Germans included Japan, Turkey, and Rumania.

Another application of the theory can be made to advancement within bureaucratic organizations. Persons above and below any given position correspond to neighbors and, according to the theory, will be enemies; persons two spots above and two spots below such a position will be friends. To illustrate, the vice-president of a firm may be able to replace the president by gaining the favor of the chairman of the board. The president, in turn, can protect himself from this threat by obtaining damaging information from the staff of the vice-president.

A third application can be drawn from the observation that politicians who are not in power can engineer a takeover of the government by bypassing the generals and forming coalitions with the colonels. The generals, in turn, can protect themselves by obtaining treasonous information about the colonels from the captains.

6.3   BALANCE OF TRADE POLICY

The mercantilists believed that the accumulation of gold was a laudable national goal. However, it should be obvious that not every country in the world can successfully pursue this objective if the world gold supply is fixed: What one country gains, another loses. The perpetual scramble to run export surpluses is a self-defeating prospect among trading countries. Although it may make sense for countries to accumulate gold for international transaction purposes, it makes no sense for them to overaccumulate (just as an individual consumer is foolish to try to maintain excessive cash balances in his pocket). Competition for reserves in a fixed exchange rate world has been translated into competitive devaluation of currencies with the advent of floating rates.

Differential Income Elasticities (Houthakker-Magee)

It is difficult to explain why trade balances rise and fall. One hypothesis is that a trade balance can be expected to decline for a country with a high propensity to consume foreign goods relative to foreigners' propensities to consume that country's goods. In this latter case, the United States and Britain have both been found to have significantly higher import elasticities of demand than the income elasticities of their exports. The reverse is true for Japan. It is not clear why this should be the case since the United States exports high-technology goods, which should have high-income elasticities, and imports many standardized goods and necessities, which one might think would have low-income elasticities. However, the income elasticities for U.S. exports and imports of finished manufactures shown in Table 6.2 are the reverse of this. In any case, the differential-elasticities hypothesis has successfully explained the secular decline in the U.S. trade balance since 1964.

The Monetary Model

The monetary model of the trade balance suggests that the supply and demand for money should be investigated to explain trade imbalance. In a general equilibrium model, if a country wants to acquire goods, it must give up money. If it wishes to acquire more money, it must give up goods. Thus, if we know what the excess supply and demand for money is, then we can determine a residually excess supply or demand for goods. For example, if the demand for money grows by 10 percent in the United States but the supply of money grows by 20 percent, there will be an excess supply of money. This money can be decumulated through the acquisition of foreign goods, which means that the U.S. will run a trade balance deficit. While the model requires significant modification to apply to a large reserve-currency

Table 6.2 Elasticities of real U.S. imports with respect to real income (Y) and relative prices (P)*

Study and period of estimation	Crude materials		Crude foodstuffs		Manufactured food		Semi-manufactures		Finished manufactures		Total trade	
	Y	P	Y	P	Y	P	Y	P	Y	P	Y	P
1. Ball and Marwah (1962) (quarterly, 1948–58)	0.87	−0.26	0.49	−0.34	0.96	−1.87	1.22	−1.38	2.47	−3.50		
2. Rhomberg and Boissonneault (1965) (quarterly, 1948–61)	0.62	−0.21	0.60	−1.10	3.00	−2.30	0.93	−0.73	0.58	−0.48		
3. Kreinin (1967) (annual, 1954–1964)			0.27	−0.40	0.60	−1.67	1.05	−0.61	2.25	−5.03		
4. Houthakker and Magee (1969) (quarterly, 1947–66)												
a. Short-run	0.18	−0.05	0.12	−0.09	0.47	−0.51	0.14	−0.18	0.29	−0.45	0.33	−0.20
b. Long-run	0.61	−0.18	0.30	−0.21	1.28	−1.40	1.11	−1.83	2.63	−4.05	1.42	−0.88
5. Magee (1970) (annual, 1951–69)												
a. U.S. imports	0.72		0.05	−0.40	1.39	−1.14	1.38	−0.78	2.45	−5.02	1.45	−1.35
b. U.S. exports	1.06	−1.21	0.36	−2.09	0.87	−2.62	1.62		1.44	−1.76	1.45	−2.00

*All are for imports except Magee (1970), which gives both exports and imports.
Source: Magee (1975, p. 182)

country such as the United States, the monetary model has provided good explanations of the balance of payments of smaller countries such as Australia, Japan, and Sweden. However, it is more difficult to use the model without considerable modification to explain trade balances.

Purchasing-Power Parity

Regardless of the cause, disequilibria are reflected in prices. If the price of goods in the United States exceeds the exchange rate and transportation cost adjusted price of the same goods abroad, then U.S. goods are said to be *overvalued*. This puts pressure on markets such that the United States will wish to increase its purchase of foreign goods and sell fewer goods to foreigners. Thus there is a natural equilibrating mechanism that causes disequilibria to be eventually eliminated. There is some evidence that the dollar was undervalued in the early 1960s and overvalued in the late 1960s. For a specific example, consider U.S. imports of certain steel plates from Japan. U.S. prices were 20 percent below Japanese prices in the early '60s, and almost 20 percent higher than Japanese prices in the late 1960s (see Fig. 6.2). Thus the trade balance could be expected to strengthen in a period of currency undervaluation and weaken in a period of currency overvaluation. Several examples of the failure of purchasing-power parity to hold for wines and taxicab rides were provided in Chapter 1 in the discussion of the law of one price.

Trade Balances, Politics, and the Opium Wars

The Opium Wars between Britain and China in the 1830s and 1850s illustrate several principles relating international trade, domestic politics, and failure of the adjustment mechanism. In 1599, the East India Company was granted a legal monopoly over trade between Britain and the subcontinents of India and China. The Company imported raw silk, porcelain, rhubarb, camphor, spices, jewels, ivory, and tin into Britain and exported largely specie (gold, silver, bullion, and coin) in payment for these items. In the 1700s, two developments altered this pattern of trade. First, British textile manufacturers induced Parliament to restrict East India Company imports of calicos, wrought silks, muslins, and other fabrics into Britain. British industry in this area was underdeveloped and the industry was not able to survive without artificial protection. The debates over these restrictions provide an early example of the infant-industry argument for protection. The East India Company lost a profitable piece of its trade with these restrictions and sought another product to replace textiles on shipments from the Far East to Britain.

The second important development was the Company's decision to replace its lost textile trade with tea. Tea was not widely consumed in

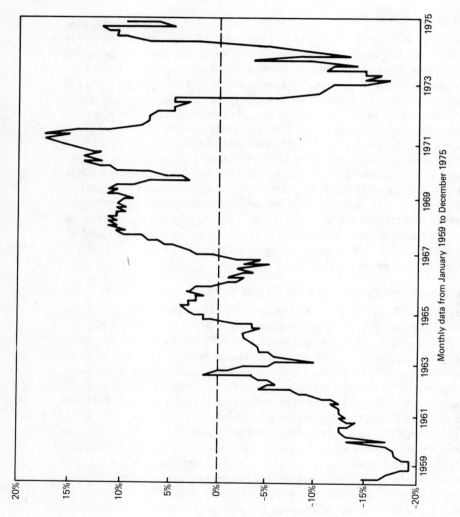

Fig. 6.2   Percentage excess of US over Japanese Prices for steel plates, 1959–1975

Monthly data from January 1959 to December 1975

Britain at that time, but it appeared promising. The Company began to increase its shipments of tea from China. In 1784, the British government reduced duties on tea from over 100 percent to 12 1/2 percent. Removal of these restrictions did not meet the usual political resistance since there was no British tea industry. In fact, the East India Company's campaign to get Britons to drink tea was so successful that Parliament eventually passed an act requiring that the Company keep a mimimum of one year's supply of tea in stock. The growing taste for tea led to an increasing payments imbalance with China, which could only be paid in specie. (China was reluctant to import other goods in payment for the tea.) Furthermore, early attempts by the British to grow tea outside of China were unsuccessful. (They succeeded in growing tea in India in the 1820s, but it was many years before this venture became commercially important.)

Nearly two centuries of paying the Chinese in specie began to erode the British supply of coin. Data from the first half of the 1700s indicate that exports from Britain to the East were over 74 percent in "treasure" and only about 36 percent in goods. From 1792 to 1807 exports from Britain to Canton equalled only 16.6 million pounds, while British imports from Canton equalled 27.2 million. There was considerable criticism of the East India Company's export of treasure from Britain. The mercantilist and bullionist theories that a country's wealth could be measured in terms of the amount of gold and specie it possessed was frequently used as an argument to criticize the East India Company's monopoly. The problem was accentuated toward the end of the 1700s as British consumption of tea grew even more rapidly and as the market for Spanish dollars was closed off when Spain entered the American War of Independence.

Again, the East India Company found a solution to the trade imbalance. Although China strongly opposed drug imports, there was a black market there where opium could be exchanged for tea, and opium was available in India. The Company discovered that it could ship manufactures from Britain to India, opium from India to China, and tea from China to Britain. By 1828, over 70 percent of the shipments from India to China were opium. These developments reversed the flow of treasure from Britain to the East: From 1818 to 1833 only about one-fifth of the British exports to the East were treasure. Frustration by the Chinese government at its inability to stop the opium trade led to the first Opium War between Britain and China from 1839 to 1842. Even though China lost the war, the result was inconclusive since it still refused to legalize the opium trade. Fifteen years later, another Opium War was fought, followed by legalized cultivation of opium in China.

This chronology provides three points. First, political limitation of British textile imports led to a trade imbalance. The solution to this imbalance was found by a powerful company, which stimulated the tastes of the population for foreign goods. By stimulating the British demand for tea, the East India Company eventually recouped its losses by replacing textiles with tea, a totally different commodity. Similarly, when pressures developed on the Company to reduce the flow of gold and silver to China, it responded by stimulating a Chinese taste for an addictive commodity. The moral seems to be that when powerful market forces exist for trade, government barriers to such trade will eventually break down.

Second, when a country such as China attempts to run a persistent trade balance surplus, forces are generated which will undo such a policy. While trade imbalances among countries generate conflicts even today, they do not usually lead to war.

Third, a country does not have to balance its trade with each partner individually in order to be in overall balance: If the deficits with one country are offset by surpluses with others, equilibrium can exist. For example, Britain exported manufactures to India, which exported opium to China, which exported tea to Britain. If none of the three countries had an overall imbalance, such a trading pattern today would be called a *trilateral balance*.

6.4 ECONOMIC IMPERIALISM

Theories of imperialism attempt to explain the economic expansion of nation states. Imperialism involves interactions among states with the relationships characterized by dominance, unequal exchange, and exploitation. If we exclude Schumpeter's view that expansionism occurred at random or is irrational behavior, there are at least four such theories.

The Underconsumption Theory

Sismondi, a Swiss historian, and Rodbertus, a German, developed the underconsumption theory, arguing that developed capitalistic economies suffer from a permanently widening gap between effective demand and production: They produce more than they can consume. As declining rates of profit reduce the opportunity for profitable employment of labor, the competition among workers for scarce jobs pulls down wages and diminishes domestic purchasing power.

Hobson is the father of the underconsumption hypothesis as the explanation for imperialism. He argued that excessive savings causes an overaccumulation of capital, which causes entrepreneurs to look for foreign markets in which to sell their goods. Hobson viewed the export of capital in the form of monopolized foreign markets as inevitable. Lenin combined Hobson's and Hilferding's dynamics of financial capital to postulate that imperialism is a higher state of capitalism. Lenin did not emphasize the lack of investment opportunities at home as the main source of expansion; rather, he claimed that it is the international competition between capitalist economies that creates the need for capital export, implemented via control over markets and resources overseas.

The Theory of Export Monopoly

Hilferding first developed the *finance capital theory of imperialism*. There are several steps in this theory. first, tariffs change from a device of protection from foreigners to a vehicle for cartel formation. The monopolies thus formed are driven to gain control over foreign markets since the protectionism prevents free competition for the factors of production. Finally, emergence of the cartels is accompanied by concentration in banking: Interest rates are held above the true scarcity value of money, leaving capital idle and creating an interest in more profitable investments abroad. In contrast to the underconsumption theorists, Hilferding identifies the capital export as the path breaker for the commodity exports. The role of the state is crucial in Hilferding's theory: He, like Hobson, claims that the states serve as a risk-minimizing investment shield.

In sum, Hilferding establishes a causal chain which runs from tariffs to monopolization to imperialism. The general explanatory capacity of Hilferding's theory is limited. Britain's imperialism deviates from his pattern: During the period of the scramble for Africa, Britain supported free trade so that trust and cartel formation was negligible. Furthermore, this state-supported monopolization of the Hilferding kind had occurred already in precapitalistic societies of the 16th and 17th centuries. Finally, the theory is weak today since the interests pressing for protection in the United States have almost no desire to stimulate U.S. exports.

The Keynesian Theory

Keynesian economics provides an explanation for imperialism which runs counter to the Marxists. Allocation decisions, like investments, have to be made in the "nowhere land" between an irrevocable past and an uncertain future, meaning historical events are terrible predictors of future events. Occasionally, the expected return on investments becomes so unfavorable that people start to hoard the capital. The resulting stagnation is called a *liquidity trap*. The only way to get the economy out of the slump is to change the preference for liquidity and stimulate dishoarding. This can be done by building pyramids, cathedrals, highways, etc.; stocking up military hardware; going to war; investing in commercial adventures; and supporting colonization. Thus, imperialism in the form of colonialism, or more subtle forms of exploitation, is one of the ways out of an investment stagnation.

The Unequal Exchange Theory

Emmanuel, a present-day Marxist, suggests that the gap between the rich and poor countries is due to a continuous "unequal exchange in international trade." More is given for less in terms of product-embodied labor time. If labor is internationally immobile, we observe that there is an international equalization of profit rates, but not an equalization of wage rates. The differences in wage rates are not a function of productivities of labor; the exact opposite is true. The result is that a worker-hour of labor from a developed country is worth more on world markets than that from underdeveloped countries.

The law of comparative costs, in contrast, dictates that gains are to be made if each country specializes according to its comparative advantage, and total world output will rise with trade. Even if Emmanuel is correct that an exploitative country reaps 90 percent of the gain while the other gets 10 percent, this does not mean that one party loses from trade. Emmanuel confuses an unequal distribution of the *gains* from trade with *absolute changes* in welfare.

6.5 INTERNATIONAL TRADE AND ECONOMIC DEVELOPMENT

The developing countries are frustrated at not having achieved the levels of economic development they had thought possible in the early postwar period. While they have recently received favorable tariff concessions ("tariff preference") by the developed countries, their exports have not been stimulated significantly. *Tariff preference* means that the developed countries charge lower tariffs on imports from developing countries for certain manufactured goods than they charge on the same imports from other developed countries. However, since tariff rates tend to be low on these items anyway, and many important commodities of importance in developing-country exports are excluded from preferential treatment, we turn to two other issues.

One of the most important features of the growth experienced by the present high-income countries has been the expansion of their manufactures. We shall explore here the relationship between manufactured exports and economic development. We shall also examine the relationship between fluctuations in export earnings and the economic development process. Developing countries frequently complain that the large fluctuations in their exports retard their economic development. Although this argument is theoretically correct, it is not always easy to prove.

Manufactured Exports and Development

Maizel reports that most of the developing countries today are still at a lower level of technological development than most European countries and Japan were at the turn of this century. At that time the share of manufacturers in total exports were 46 percent for France, 70 percent for Germany, 41 percent for Italy, 30 percent for Sweden, 75 percent for Switzerland, and 42 percent for Japan. However, the share of manufactured exports in total exports of developing countries has increased from about 7 percent in 1953 to a little over 20 percent just before the oil price rise. While the raw material advantage of today's developing countries causes this number to be artificially low, it is nevertheless true that they have a long way to go. For example, the technological gap between developed and developing countries is greater today than it was between most European countries and the United States in 1900.

One reason for these results is that today's developing countries adopted an active policy of import substitution in the 1960s. Instead of concentrating on stimulation of exports, developing countries attempted to reduce their dependence on manufactured imports by imposing high tariffs and introducing other restrictive policies. Table 6.3 compares the average nominal tariff rates for 17 of today's developed countries in the year 1902 with the average tariff rates in 18 developing countries in the 1970s. Observe that the developing countries' average tariff of 62 percent is considerably higher than the average of 27 percent in 1902 for today's developed countries.

What patterns emerge for successful export of manufactures by today's developing countries?

Morrison's study of manufacturing exports of developing countries finds that they are positively correlated with the population of the exporting country, its income per capita, and the population density of the exporting country and negatively related to the percentage of the population that is literate. Population is a proxy for domestic market size in the exporting country. The hypothesis is that larger countries will be better able to exploit economies of scale and have more competition, thus permitting greater specialization of economic functions. Income per capita reflects the level of economic development of the exporting country since it will be correlated with efficient infrastructure, management skills, and other attributes necessary for effective competition in world trade. The population density variable is explained by the fact that densely populated countries tend to specialize in manufactures, while sparsely populated countries tend to specialize in primary and land-intensive products. While the negative correlation between manufactured exports and literacy is puzzling, it may be explained by speciali-

Table 6.3   Average tariff rates (percent)

Average tariff rates in 1902		Average tariff rates, 1970s	
Spain	76	Uruguay	184
United States	73	Chile	166
Portugal	71	Brazil	96
France	34	Pakistan	85
Italy	27	Ecuador	81
Germany	25	Argentina	74
Sweden	23	Peru	63
Denmark	18	Colombia	49
Canada	17	Venezuela	45
Belgium	13	Turkey	44
Norway	12	Korea	35
New Zealand	9	Israel	32
Japan	9	Taiwan	30
Switzerland	7	Bolivia	26
Australia	6	Tanzania	26
Netherlands	3	Philippines	25
		Mexico	24
		Malasia	10
Average	27	Average	62

Source: Morrison, 1976, p. 51.

zation of developing countries in manufactured goods which are unskilled-labor intensive in production.

A most important implication for international commercial policy is that the level of manufactured exports of a developing country was negatively correlated with its tariff rate on imports. This conforms to our expectations since high tariffs on imports cause import-competing production to be more profitable. This encourages resources to move from export activities into import-competing activities and retards the ability of the economy to exploit its comparative advantage through exports.

Fluctuations in Export Earnings in Developing Countries

One of the widely discussed problems of the developing countries is the instability of their export proceeds. Table 6.4 shows that the average percentage deviation of the dollar value of exports around a 5-year moving average (i.e., the average value of exports 2 years before, in the same year, and 2 years following) is higher for underdeveloped countries than for developed countries. The average percentage deviation was 23 percent for the developing countries and only 18 percent for developed countries.

Some of the traditionally accepted explanations for this behavior include the tendency of developing countries to export mainly primary products, a tendency for them to concentrate their exports on a relatively few number of products and a tendency for their exports to be concentrated in a fairly limited number of purchasing countries. However, MacBean (1966) showed that none of these three explanations can be statistically associated with the export fluctuations in the developing countries. Considerable controversy exists on these questions; however, some empirical tests of commodity agreements have confirmed the explanatory power of these traditional variables (see Chapter 4).

Table 6.4   Instability indices for exports

Developing countries		Developed countries	
Argentina	41%	Australia	25%
Bolivia	27	Austria	21
Brazil	14	Belgium-Luxembourg	18
Burma	15	Canada	7
Ceylon (Sri Lanka)	13	Denmark	10
Chile	20	Finland	30
Taiwan	16	France	21
Colombia	13	West Germany	19
Costa Rica	14	Iceland	22
Cuba	26	Ireland	6
Dominican Republic	17	Israel	12
Ecuador	25	Italy	21
Egypt	20	Japan	31
El Salvador	14	Norway	16
Ethiopia-Eritrea	24	Sweden	15
Ghana	32	Switzerland	6
Greece	18	United Kingdom	18
Guatemala	11	United States	17
Haiti	27		
Honduras	16	Average	18
India	16	Standard	
Indonesia	57	Deviation	(7)
Iran	74		
Iraq	27		
Malaya	42		
Mexico	11		
Morocco	26		
Nicaragua	14		
Nigeria	21		
Pakistan	36		

Table 6.4   (continued)

Developing countries		Developed countries
Panama	10	
Paraguay	16	
Peru	10	
Philippines	18	
Portugal	15	
Rhodesia-Nyasaland	12	
Sudan	40	
Syria	16	
Thailand	37	
Tunisia	33	
Turkey	19	
Union of S. Africa	10	
Uruguay	20	
Venezuela	16	
Vietnam	38	
Average	23	
Standard Deviation	(13)	

Source: MacBean (1966, pp. 37 and 40). The instability measure is the average absolute percentage deviation of exports from a five-year moving average of exports.

A more important result is MacBean's finding that the economic performance of many developing countries is unrelated to their instability of exports. That is, countries with high export instability do not have poorer economic performance. He found little evidence that income movements are closely related to fluctuations in export earnings. In fact, a number of countries with highly unstable exports have relatively stable incomes. He attributes this result to the failure of exports to have a very large multiplier effect on economic behavior in the developing countries. Furthermore, MacBean found no support for the idea that export instability reduces capital formation. His careful examination of twelve underdeveloped countries which experienced high export instability over the period from 1946 to 1958 leads to the result that there were frequent quite specific "local" causes of economic difficulties in each case. These include national economic policies, wars, and civil strife.

REFERENCES

1. Balassa, Bela, *The Theory of Economic Integration.* Homewood, Ill.: Richard D. Irwin, 1961.

2. Barratt Brown, M., *The Economics of Imperialism.* London: Penguin, 1974.

3. Brock, William A. and Magee, Stephen P., "The Economics of Special-Interest Politics: The Case of the Tariff," *American Economic Review* **68** (May 1978): 246–250.

4. ———, "Tariff Setting in a Democracy," in Black, John and Hindley, Brian, eds., *Current Issues in International Commercial Policy and Economic Diplomacy,* London: Macmillan Press, 1979.

5. Caves, Richard E. and Jones, Ronald W., *World Trade in Payments.* Boston: Little, Brown & Company, 2nd edition, 1977.

6. Corden, W.M., *Trade Policy and Economic Welfare.* Oxford: Clarendon, 1974.

7. Frenkel, Jacob and Johnson, Harry G., *The Monetary Approach to the Balance of Payments.* Toronto: University of Toronto Press, 1976.

8. Greenberg, Michael, *British Trade and the Opening of China 1800–42.* Cambridge: Cambridge University Press, 1951.

9. Houthakker, Hendrik S. and Magee, Stephen P., "Income and Price Elasticities in World Trade," *Review of Economics and Statistics* **51** (May 1969): 111–125.

10. MacBean, Alistair, *Export Instability and Economic Development.* London: Allen & Unwin, 1966.

11. Magee, Stephen P., "The Welfare Effects of Restrictions on U.S. Trade," *Brookings Papers on Economic Activity* (No. 3, 1972): 645–701.

12. ———, "Prices, Incomes and Foreign Trade," in Kenen, Peter B., ed., *International Trade and Finance: Frontiers for Research.* New York: Cambridge University Press, 1975: 175–252.

13. ———, *Empirical Essays in Internation Trade,* forthcoming.

14. Maizel, A., *Exports and Economic Growth of Developing Countries.* Cambridge: Cambridge University Press, 1968.

15. Morrison, Thomas K., *Manufactured Exports for Developing Countries.* New York: Praeger, 1976.

16. Verdoorn, P.J., "Two Notes on Tariff Reductions," in *Social Aspects of European Economic Cooperation,* International Labour Office, Geneva, 1956.

Index

93